An intro(psy holo(...les

2nd edition

In its first edition this book successfully enabled readers, with little or no prior knowledge of computing or statistics, to develop reliable and valid tests and scales for assessment or research purposes. In this edition, the author has thoroughly updated the text to include new recent advances in computer software and provide information on relevant internet resources. The book contains detailed guidelines for locating and constructing psychological measures, including descriptions of popular psychological measures and step-by-step instructions for composing a measure, entering data, and computing reliability and validity of test results. Advanced techniques such as factor analysis, analysis of covariance and multiple regression analysis are presented for the beginner.

An Introduction to Psychological Tests and Scales provides a clear, concise and jargon-free primer for all those embarking on field-work or research analysis. It will be an invaluable tool for undergraduates and postgraduates in psychology and a useful text for students and professionals in related disciplines.

Kate Loewenthal is Professor of Psychology at Royal Holloway College, University of London.

An introduction to psychological tests and scales

2nd edition

Kate Miriam Loewenthal

Royal Holloway
University of London

First published 2001 by Psychology Press Ltd
27 Church Road, Hove, East Sussex, BN3 2FA

http://www.psypress.co.uk

Simultaneously published in the USA and Canada
by Taylor & Francis Inc.,
325 Chestnut Street, Philadelphia, PA 19106

Psychology Press is a part of the Taylor & Francis Group

British Library Cataloguing in Publication Data
A catalogue record for this book is available from the British Library

ISBN 1-84169-106-2 (hbk)
ISBN 1-84169-139-9 (pbk)

Library of Congress Cataloging in Publication Data

Loewenthal, Kate Miriam.
    An introduction to psychological tests and scales / Kate Miriam
Loewenthal. – 2nd ed.
        p. cm.
    Includes bibliographical references and index.
    ISBN 1-84169-106-2 – ISBN 1-84169-139-9 (pbk.)
    1. Psychological tests. I. Title.

    BF176 .L64 2001
    150'.28'7–dc21   00-062772

Cover design by Sandra Heath
Typeset in Times by Mayhew Typesetting, Rhayader, Powys
Printed and bound in Great Britain by TJ International Ltd, Padstow,
Cornwall, UK

Contents

Foreword		viii
Preface		x
Acknowledgements		xii
1	**What is a good psychological measure?**	1
	The aims of this book	1
	Features of good psychological measures	2
	Summary	20
2	**A guide to finding and using existing tests and scales**	21
	Finding the scale	22
	Pros and cons of using an existing scale	28
	Using the scale	28
	Summary	29
3	**Writing**	30
	Defining what you want to measure	30
	Collecting items	32
	Producing the preliminary questionnaire or test	35
	Summary	41
4	**Testing**	42
	Deciding on a sample and reducing sample bias	42
	Recruiting methods	48
	Testing	50
	Summary	52
5	**Data and preliminary analysis**	53
	Coding, scoring, and data entry	53

Selecting reliable items   59
Descriptive statistics (norms) for the final scale   64
Summary of steps for data entry and reliability   64
Factor and principal components analyses   65
Summary   67

6   The final scale and its validation   68
Descriptive statistics (norms)   68
Validity   68
Presenting the scale   75
Summary   76

APPENDICES

Appendix to Chapter 1
Examples of test and scale presentation   77
   Example 1. Narcissistic Personality Inventory (NPI)   77
   Example 2. Individual Responsibility (IR) measure   79
   Example 3. Structure of Prayer Scale   82
   Example 4. Quality of Cognitive Therapy Scale (CTS)   83

Appendix to Chapter 2
Selecting tests   86
   2.1   Guidelines for psychological testing   86
   2.2   Publishers of psychological tests   91
   2.3   Measures included in the National Foundation for Educational Research (NFER) portfolios   92
   2.4   The British Psychological Society's Certificates of Competence in Occupational Testing   97
   2.5   Some useful tests: An introductory review   98

Appendix to Chapter 4
Ethical guidelines   114
   4.1   The Australian Psychological Society's Guidelines for the use of Psychological tests   114
   4.2   Conducting an individual testing session   116
   4.3   Feedback   116
   4.4   Ethical Committee of Royal Holloway University of London: Notes for guidance   117
   4.5   Guidelines for medical research   118

Appendix to Chapter 5
Reliability 119
   5.1   *Types of data, coding, and statistics* 120
   5.2   *An example of coding* 122
   5.3   *Making and checking a database in SPSS for*
        Windows 124
   5.4   *Reliability analysis in SPSS for Windows* 133
   5.5   *Improving reliability* 135
   5.6   *Factor and principal components analyses in SPSS*
        for Windows 138

Appendix to Chapter 6
Computation and validity 143
   6.1   *Computing total scores on your measure* 143
   6.2   *Criterion validity using an unrelated t-test* 144
   6.3   *Concurrent validity: Using SPSS to calculate*
        correlations 147
   6.4   *Criterion and predictive validity: One-way analysis*
        of variance in SPSS, including comparisons
        between groups 149
   6.5   *Confounded variables: Loglinear analysis, logistic*
        regression, analysis of covariance, and multiple
        regression analysis 152

   Bibliography 155
   Useful web sites 163
   Author index 165
   Subject index 168

Foreword

It is extremely important for psychologists to have available to them adequate measuring instruments. In several areas of psychology (e.g., social psychology; personality; intelligence) these measuring instruments often take the form of psychological tests and scales. However, most of the authors of books dealing specifically with psychological test construction and evaluation assume that their readers possess great statistical expertise and considerable prior knowledge of psychology. In my experience, this is a dubious assumption to make about academic psychologists, and is wholly unwarranted so far as undergraduate students are concerned!

What Kate Loewenthal has attempted to do (and has succeeded admirably in doing) is to write a book on psychological tests and scales that is accessible and readily comprehensible by those lacking confidence in their understanding of statistics. This accessibility is achieved in part through the clarity and coherence of the writing style. It is also achieved by providing basic guidance on how to construct tests and evaluate their reliability and validity, rather than by focusing on complex and abstract statistical principles.

There are other ways in which Kate Loewenthal's book makes a valuable and distinctive contribution. For example, the number of psychological tests is increasing almost on a daily basis, so that by now there must be several thousand tests available for use by psychologists. However, the key issue of how to find the test that one needs among this myriad of tests is ignored in most other books. Kate Loewenthal provides a number of eminently sensible suggestions as to ways of tracking down any given test.

In sum, Kate Loewenthal has done an outstanding job of producing a user-friendly account of what is involved in test construction and evaluation. All the stages of finding, choosing, and developing tests and scales are discussed carefully and in detail. As one would expect in this day and age, the book provides detailed instructions on the use of modern statistical software offering reliability and other relevant facilities. The only danger is that Kate Loewenthal may have made the task of test construction too easy for the thousands of readers who will read this book, as a consequence of which the steady trickle of new tests may turn into a downpour! However, that is a risk well worth taking for a book that will rapidly become an indispensable addition to the book-shelves of most psychologists and psychology students.

Michael W. Eysenck

Preface

This book aims to meet the need for an introductory text covering the basics of psychological test and scale construction. It should meet the initial needs of psychology undergraduates learning this aspect of research methods. The book could be used by other social scientists in research methods training. In addition, it opens the possibility that professionals in business and management who wish to develop tests and other instruments for selection, survey, or development purposes could use this book to achieve better standards of clarity, reliability, and validity.

The development of statistical packages incorporating a facility for measuring test reliability means that the important statistics needed for test development can be fairly easily carried out without having to spend too much time mastering basic statistics. This book is aimed at assisting in the use of computer software facilities for reliability analysis, particularly SPSS for Windows. It outlines the main stages in test and scale construction, and describes how to implement these.

There are several books on the market which deal with psychometrics—which is the theory and practice of psychological test construction. Almost all such books are unnecessarily detailed and too advanced for introductory undergraduate use, and cannot be recommended to the average undergraduate or other person who is seeking to grasp the basic principles of test construction. Although there are good, short research methods handbooks, there is no current basic handbook on psychometrics apart from Jackson (1996) and Kline (1986). The latter is excellent but now somewhat dated. The former does not offer guidance about test construction.

Throughout the book, the traditional terms "test", "scale", and "measure" have been used almost interchangeably. Nowadays the range of psychological states and constructs that is measured is widening the whole time, and the distinction between these "test", "scale", and "measure" may be harder to maintain than in the past.

"Testing" has traditionally involved comparing performance on the measuring instrument (the test) against standard performances on that instrument. The standard performance ("norm") is the average performance score on the test achieved by people from a specified group. Test scores may be "higher" or "lower" than each other. A psychological or mental test is defined by English and English (1958, p. 547) as:

> A set of standardised or controlled occasions for response presented to an individual with design to elicit a representative sample of his behaviour when meeting a given kind of environmental demand. The occasion for response most often takes the form of a question or similar verbal stimulus.

"Scaling" involves ordering and comparison of performances on the measuring instrument (the scale), without any (absolute) standards necessarily involved. English and English (1958, p. 474) defined a scale as:

> A series of test items, tasks or questions, each of which has been given a number or score value on the basis of empirical evidence of their average difficulty for a certain group of people.

Many examples of measures of psychological states, of performances and abilities, of beliefs and attitudes, of cognitions and cognitive styles, of preferences, and of personality would be hard to classify firmly as tests or scales.

The terms "person", "participant", "testee", and "respondent" have also been used fairly interchangeably. Each term has its specialist contexts: The participant is a person who participates in a psychological investigation, often an experiment. The term "participant" is recommended as a substitute for "subject". "Subject" is now viewed by the American Psychological Association and the British Psychological Society as not politically correct. The testee is the person tested (usually by a psychologist), whereas the respondent (or interviewee) is the person questioned (usually by a social scientist or survey worker). Readers from different academic or professional backgrounds may prefer one term to others.

This book seeks to convey some basic principles and methods of psychological test and scale construction—not only to those who know they need them, but also to those who should or could be using them but who have not and cannot use them because of their inaccessibility.

ACKNOWLEDGEMENTS

Many thanks to my family for being so patient and supportive while I gave attention to this book, especially to my husband Tali Loewenthal, and my children (Esther, Leah, Yitzi, Chana-Soro, Moshe, Rivky, Brocha, Freidy, Sholi, Mendy, and Zalmy), sons-in-law, daughters-in-law, and grandchildren, and to the Lubavitcher Rebbe.

In addition to those who read and commented on the first edition of this book, to whom I remain very thankful, the following read and made very helpful comments on drafts of this edition: Christopher Alan Lewis (University of Ulster), Davis Clark-Carter, and Duncan Cramer (Loughborough University). Thanks to Rosemary Westley, Mary Atkins, Brooke Rogers, and other colleagues (Royal Holloway University of London) for their many kind acts of help, particularly chasing up details of tests and related material needed for this book, and also to Rachel Brazil, Alison Dixon, Kathryn Russel and others at Psychology Press for their advice and support.

Chapter 1

What is a good psychological measure?

THE AIMS OF THIS BOOK

This book aims to offer a step-by-step guide to finding and constructing a reliable and valid measure of a psychological factor. This chapter describes the properties of good psychological measures.

The psychological factor might be a reported state of mind—emotion or attitude, for example—or it might be reported behaviour. Thus the book introduces its readers to the use and production of a psychological scale, test, or measure. It is not a comprehensive manual, but a guide for those who have never attempted test or scale construction before, and who may have limited experience in finding and using psychological measures. The book outlines the principles and practices involved.

Those most likely to find the book useful are undergraduates or postgraduates in psychology or behavioural science. The book may also be useful to those working in education, health, business, and industry. The book is intended as a guide for novices. Some background in statistics and computing would be an advantage though not absolutely essential.

The book will enable you to:

- construct simple self-report measures of psychological constructs, such as beliefs, attitudes, moods, feelings, values, intentions, behaviour, knowledge, and skills.

Additionally, it should improve your ability to:

- report on the use of any existing measure;
- describe and evaluate any existing measure;
- understand others' reports, descriptions, and evaluations;
- select a test for use from those already in existence.

It is however an *introductory* book, and deals chiefly with measures of a *single* psychological factor, using a uniform type of test item, enabling scores to be obtained by adding. The procedures involved in standardising test scores are not covered. Use Anastasi and Urbina (1996), Kaplan and Saccuzzo (2000), or Kline (1986, 1993, 1999), for coverage of this topic. For more elaborate tests, and for designing tests for use in specialist contexts (such as clinical diagnosis), you would need to use a more specialist book. Cohen (1999), Gregory (1996), Groth-Marnat (1997), and Kaplan and Saccuzzo (2000) are useful general guides to psychological assessment in different contexts, which treat the topic in greater breadth and depth than is possible here.

A warning: the detailed instructions for computing using SPSS, and the web addresses offered in this book, are accurate at the time of writing. However SPSS is frequently updated, and web sites are sometimes dismantled. Most or all of the information in the book will be helpful, but be alert for difficulties which might be caused by changes.

We turn now to defining the features of good psychological measures.

FEATURES OF GOOD PSYCHOLOGICAL MEASURES

Look out for the following features—and if you are developing a measure yourself, use this as a check list of features to include:

- a statement of what the scale measures;
- justification for the scale—its uses, and advantages over existing measures;
- a description of how the preliminary pool of items was drawn up;
- a description of the sample used for testing;

- an indication of the populations (kinds of people) for whom the measure would be appropriate;
- descriptive statistics (norms): means, standard deviations, ranges, different subscales;
- reliability statistics;
- validity statistics;
- the scale itself (instructions, items, or examples of items).

Appendix 1 describes several examples of presentation. Look there to see examples of how presentation is carried out in practice. The text that follows elaborates on this list of features.

A statement of what the scale measures

This would not normally be very long. However it is often difficult to produce. The reason for the difficulty is that one is required to formulate and define the obvious! Try to formulate this statement very early in the development of any scale. Preferably it should be the first thing you do, if you are producing a scale.

Justification for the scale

The scale's background and history, including underlying theory, its uses, and advantages over existing measures should be explained.

You may need to include a rationale for having a scale at all, rather than a single-item measure. For example, explaining why you need 20 or 30 questions looking at different facets of belief about prayer, or different symptoms of depressive illness, rather than just one question asking for an indication of favourability to prayer, or extent of depression. Typically, a multi-item measure is needed where there is an underlying central conceptual entity, with a number of facets, which may not be tapped by a single question. In the case of depression, for example, depressed mood, suicide plans, sleep disturbance, and so forth do not always go along with each other, and could not be tapped with single question.

How the preliminary pool of items was drawn up

Give details of the sources used, how if at all they were sampled, and any special steps taken to check the wording of the items. For example you might describe how you asked, say, three people to read the items to check for meaning, clarity, ambiguity, and double-barrelled-ness, and then report that you made amendments in the light of their comments.

Description of the sample used for testing

Any psychological test or measure should be presented with a description of the group or groups of people who did the test and contributed to the mean score(s). If the test is given to different types of people, we would not necessarily expect their performances to be similar. Thus anyone using your test needs to know whether their testee came from the same population as your norming sample, in order to interpret their score(s) in the light of your norms. Any special local or historical circumstances should be noted. For example:

126 female New Zealand psychology undergraduates,
42 male first admission schizophrenics,
31 children aged 6–9 years described by their teachers as having
    reading difficulties (20 boys and 11 girls),
535 male British army recruits, tested in the 2 weeks following the
    outbreak of the Falklands war.

Mean age and age range should be given where possible, and any details of cultural background that cannot be inferred from knowing the country in which the test was carried out. Ideally, performance of males and females (and any other subgroups) should be examined separately, and if performances differ, means should be presented separately. The overall scale mean should of course be given, and, if wished, overall item mean (see the discussion that follows).

Means, standard deviations, and ranges (norms)

These should always be presented. Believe it or not, there are published tests that do not give these details, and it is very annoying to test users to discover that they are not available, because one would generally wish to compare performances of one's testees with norms.

Means and ranges (highest and lowest scores) are easy to work out. Standard deviations take a while if you are without computer software, but hopefully you will have the use of a statistical package.

The *mean* (average) is the most commonly used measure of central tendency. It is the total of everyone's total scores on the test, divided by the number of people who did the test. Some would prefer to quote an *item mean*, which is the mean score for one item (the scale mean is divided by the number of items). This has the advantage that if the number of items in the scale is varied, comparisons can still be made between people doing different versions of the scale, with different numbers of items in each version. The *standard deviation* is a measure of how much spread there is in the scores. Refer to a statistics textbook if you are interested in the details of how this is calculated. The *range* is simply the highest and the lowest score. It is a good idea to show the range actually obtained, and the theoretically possible range if this is different from the range actually obtained. For example:

Mean: 13.45
Standard deviation: 6.74
Range (obtained): 2–24; Full range: 0–25.

Reliability

Definition

Reliability is consistency. Do different bits of your measure give similar results? If you gave your measure again to the same people would they score similarly? If you gave your measure to similar people, would they score similarly? The British Psychological Society Steering Committee on Test Standards (1992, p. 6) defines reliability as "the extent to which the outcome of a test remains unaffected by irrelevant variations in the conditions and procedures of testing", and as "consistency of measurement". The British Psychological Society Steering Committee on Test Standards (1999, p. 4) says that reliability is a reflection of "how accurate or precise a test score is". A very friendly introduction to reliability and related issues appears in Gravetter and Wallnau (1999), and its associated web site (see p. 163). Here, we are instructed: "When you think about reliability, think CONSISTENCY".

There are different measures of reliability, and more is said about these different measures next. An unreliable measure is of limited value. If different questions or items on your test give inconsistent results, then you are not assessing anything. This may seem trivial, but a crucial hallmark of a good test is that you do the work necessary to establish its reliability.

Wording

A test cannot be reliable unless the items are clear and unambiguous. For example if I want to assess mood, and ask people to indicate which mood words normally apply to them, I should not normally choose words like "mad", or "favours" in my test because they have different meanings in different cultures. "Mad" denotes angry in US English, and insane in British English. "Favours" denotes preference and liking to many English-speakers, but in Jamaica it can mean "resemble". Thus some knowledge of colloquialisms can be an advantage. Again, this may seem trivial, but it is important to spend time making sure that your items really are about what you intend them to be about. A number of well-known tests fall a little short here.

Correlation

It is important to produce a numerical (statistical) measure of reliability, that is objectively defined, so as to allow comparison between tests. Measures of reliability are usually based on correlation coefficients. A correlation coefficient can range from 1.0 through 0 down to −1.0, and it is a measure of the strength of association or similarity between two sets of scores obtained by the same people. A correlation coefficient of 1.0 or nearly 1.0 means that the two sets of scores are strongly associated or very similar. A person who got a high score on one test or on one occasion also got a high score the second time; low scorers on the first set of scores were low scorers on the second set. A high negative correlation of −1.0 or nearly −1.0, means that the two sets of scores are also strongly associated but the association is negative and high scores in one set of scores go along with *low* scores in the other set, and vice versa. A correlation coefficient of 0 or nearly 0 means that the two sets of scores are not related at all: A high score in one set of scores may be associated with a high score in the other set, or a medium score, or a low score—we just cannot predict anything about scores in the second set from scores in the first set. In evaluating reliability coefficients we are usually looking for high positive values. The statistical significance of a coefficient (significance indicates the extent to which the result could be due to chance; see the discussion that follows) depends on the size of the coefficient *and* on the size of sample (of people). Figures 1.1–1.3 illustrate what various correlation coefficients indicate about the relationships between two measures.

A high positive correlation means that high values on one measure go along with high values on the other measure (Figure 1.1). A high negative correlation means that high values on one measure go along with *low* values on the other measures, and vice versa (Figure 1.2). A zero or low correlation means that you cannot tell anything about what the value on the second measure is likely to be, from knowing the value on the first measure (Figure 1.3).

If this is not old news, an example may make things clearer. Let us say I am developing a measure of trust in clinical psychologists, and I give my measure to 50 patients suffering from phobias. A week later I give the same measure to the same 50 patients. A correlation of .82 would suggest that high scores the first time

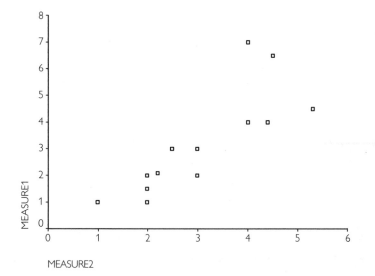

Figure 1.1 A positive correlation, $r = +.82$.

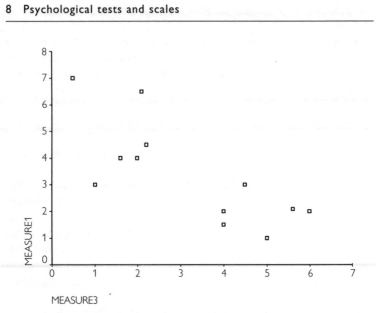

Figure 1.2   A negative correlation, *r* = −.77.

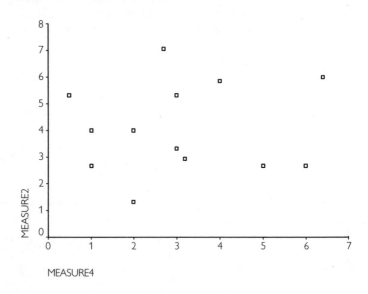

Figure 1.3   A near-zero correlation, *r* = .02.

generally went with high scores the second time. A correlation of −.77 (unlikely, but you never know) indicates that high scores the first time went with low scores the second time and vice versa—in other words, most of the patients who said they had some trust the first time, changed their minds, and so did the mistrustful patients. A correlation of, say .02 means that scores the first week predicted almost nothing about scores the second week. Only the first result—the fairly high positive correlation of .81—suggests that the test is reliable. The statistical significance of the correlation is the *probability* of getting that coefficient by chance, that is, as a result of "sampling error". Sampling error is said to have occurred when your population is not truly representative of the population it is supposed to represent. A very low probability indicates that it was very unlikely that you obtained that coefficient by chance, as a result of sampling error. A very *low* probability indicates acceptable statistical significance. Normally, probabilities of less than .05 are acceptable, at least for exploratory research and small samples; ideally they should be less than .01, especially where sample size is large. Statistical software packages will work out probabilities for you. If you are working without such a package, then statistical tables will have to be consulted. In our example, the probability of getting a correlation of .76 with a sample of 50 is much less than .01, so the result would be considered statistically significant.

However nowadays, the most popular reliability coefficient, alpha, is judged somewhat differently from other correlation coefficients used to assess reliability. The section later in this chapter, on reliability statistics, says more about this.

Note that the statistical significance of the correlation coefficient tells you nothing about the *direction* and *strength* of the association. This information is given by the coefficient itself. So you must examine the coefficient—its *size* and *direction*—to make sensible interpretations of its meaning.

Forms of reliability assessment

All forms of reliability assessment involve two or more sets of scores from the same group of people, where the scores are supposed to measure the same thing. The investigator then calculates a measure of association between the sets of scores—usually a correlation coefficient—while hoping that the measure of association indicates a good level of agreement between the scores. There are several different ways of assessing reliability, and the investigator chooses the one(s) that suits his or her needs the best. Normally, *Cronbach's coefficient alpha* is regarded as the most desirable. This coefficient takes into account all the inter-associations between all items in the scale. You will hopefully use one of the coefficients generated automatically by a computer package, and the following notes should help you to understand something of what the computer is doing for you. Consult Anastasi and Urbina (1996) or Kline (1999) for more details on the pros and cons of the different types of reliability. Gravetter and Wallnau (1999), or their web site (see p. 163), offer a more basic but very friendly introduction.

Item-total correlations

The investigator calculates the correlation (or other measure of association) between scores on each item of the test, and the total score on the test. This is done for each item in the test. Ideally the total should be the total score on the test minus the score on the item under consideration. This will yield as many correlations as there are items in the test. It tells you, for each item, how well answers to that item relate to answers to all the other items. It sounds a bit long-winded, but you probably have to do it, as it is the best way to home in on items which are not assessing the same thing as the others. When calculating Cronbach's alpha, there should be an option that will yield item-total correlations. Appendix 5.4 describes how to access this.

Test–retest reliability

The same test is given to the same people on two different occasions (this is what happened in the imaginary example of a test assessing trust in clinical psychologists). The correlation between scores on the two occasions is calculated. This form of reliability assessment is not much use if you are assessing transitory states of mind that are easily and rapidly changed (such as mood, and many beliefs, attitudes, and intentions).

Split-half reliability

The investigator selects half the items in the test at random, and calculates a total score for that half of the test, and a total score for the other half of the test. The correlation between scores on the two half-tests are then calculated. A variation on split-half reliability is *alternate-forms* reliability, in which two different versions of a test measuring the same thing are given to the same people.

Factor and principal components analysis

These are discussed later. They are used in more elaborate forms of psychometric test development than we are concerned with in this book. If this form of analysis has been done, it can be regarded as giving a kind of measure of internal consistency for each factor. There is more about this topic on page 13 and also in Chapter 5 and Appendix 5.

Inter-rater reliability

This is a special form of reliability that needs to be calculated when ratings of observed behaviour or speech are made by an observer. Reliability is assessed by calculating the extent to which another observer makes the same ratings of the same behaviour or speech. This form of inter-judge agreement can also be used to confirm whether judges think that items are about what they are supposed to be about (see the sections on content and face validity later in this chapter).

Reliability statistics

This section describes the statistics used to assess the different types of reliability defined earlier.

Measures of internal consistency

Tests developed in the last few years tend to quote computer-generated reliability statistics. The default option (i.e., what it does automatically unless you tell it to do something else) is *Cronbach's alpha* (*the alpha coefficient of reliability*). This is defined as the estimated correlation of the test with any other test of the same length with similar items (i.e., items from the same item universe) (Kline, 1986). If you want to understand how this coefficient is derived and calculated, then you could consult Anastasi and

Urbina (1996) or Kline (1999). The reliability facility on your statistics package (e.g., SPSS) will do the computation for you. Alpha should normally be at least .70 for reliability to be regarded as satisfactory. As described previously, you can also ask for more information about how each item relates to the rest of the scale: inter-item correlations, item-total correlations, and the effects on alpha of removing each item can be computed. This information is helpful if a scale or measure has poor internal consistency, because it can be used to identify which items could be removed to improve consistency. This procedure is described in Chapter 5.

There is an interesting difference between Cronbach's alpha, and other correlation-type statistics. You probably know that the acceptability of a conventional correlation coefficient is usually judged by its statistical significance, which is related to sample size. The acceptability of Cronbach's coefficient alpha is *not* determined by its statistical significance. The absolute value of .7 (or sometimes .8 or .6) is normally taken as the criterion of acceptability.

KUDER-RICHARDSON (K-R 20)

This is a coefficient that can be interpreted in exactly the same way as Cronbach's alpha. Your statistics package may calculate it for you automatically in cases where your data are dichotomous and therefore not suitable for ordinary correlation coefficients. Ordinary correlation coefficients can be calculated when people answer each item on a rating scale (say from 0 to 7), or get a score (say from 0 to 20). If they just said "yes" or "no", "agree" or "disagree", then answers would be entered on a database as 0 or 1 (or 1 or 2); the data are said to be dichotomous and the statistics package will calculate K-R 20 instead of Cronbach's alpha. As stated, it can be interpreted in the same way as Cronbach's alpha.

TEST–RETEST RELIABILITY

This would be calculated by calculating the correlation coefficient between scores on the test on two different occasions. Normally, the Pearson (bivariate) correlation would be calculated in the usual way. *Split-half reliability* is also expressed by a correlation coefficient, showing the strength of the relationship between the two halves of the test.

GUTTMAN'S COEFFICIENTS

These and other reliability statistics may be offered by your statistics package. Refer to your statistics package handbook, or to Anastasi and Urbina (1996) or Kline (1999) if you wish to discover more about them. It is probably premature for the beginner at test construction to worry about whether they are needed.

Factor and principal components analyses

The literature on test construction frequently refers to factor analysis. Factor analysis is a way of discovering statistical "factors" among a lot of test items (variables); it is a way of analysing relations between correlations, so that one can look at relations between all variables rather than just pairs. The first step is the construction of a correlation matrix showing the correlation between each variable and every other variable. West (1991) describes factor analysis as a "technique for finding a small number of underlying dimensions from among a larger number of variables". The final output of a factor analysis includes a list of factors—listed in the order in which they contribute to the variance—with "*factor loadings*" for each variable. These factor loadings show how much every variable contributes to the factor, and they can range from $+1.0$ to -1.0. Very approximately, they correspond to the item-total correlations for each factor. The researcher names each factor by examining which variables are most heavily loaded on it.

You might consider using factor analysis if you want to develop a test that is:

- assessing something complicated, in which you suspect more than one underlying factor. A variety of items are needed for assessment, they would not be well associated with each other, and a conventional reliability analysis yields poor results;
- *and* you are unsure what the underlying factors are. When you know what the different factors are, you can write a subscale to assess each, and then examine the reliabilities of each subscale. When you do not know, then factor analysis may tell you.

An example of a case for factor analysis was said to be intelligence. Researchers were unsure about the factors involved, and so intelligence tests were constructed by writing many items testing many abilities, and then subjecting performance scores to factor analysis. There has been a certain amount of controversy surrounding the applications of factor analysis to the construction of tests of intelligence, personality and the like. Factor analysis used to be a very time-consuming process in the pre-electronic era—now of course it can be done in a few seconds. Days, even weeks of work would be involved. That may have contributed to the mystique, in which proponents would seem to be claiming a special psychological status for the factors they had laboured to discover, while critics would claim that these were mere statistical artefacts without any inherent psychological reality.

Principal components analysis yields similar results to factor analysis, but gets there by a slightly different route. Instead of looking at the relations between variables, the principal components analysis starts off by looking for factors which explain as much of the variance as possible (West, 1991).

Factor analysis and principal components analyses would be appropriate in the circumstances I have described, and further (conventional) reliability statistics to establish internal consistency would normally be redundant.

More sophisticated discussions of the uses of factor analysis in test construction appear for example in Anastasi (1988), Cattell (1946), Cook (1993), Eysenck (1952), Field (2000), Kline (1999), and Tabachnick and Fidell (1996). Field's account is very user-friendly. SPSS offers factor and principal components analysis under Analyse (Statistics)/Data Reduction. SAS/SYSTAT offers factor analysis under Psychometrics. Tabachnick and Fidell include a comparison the factor and principal-components analysis facilities on different statistics packages—but sadly, nothing ,on reliability analysis. A brief outline of factor analysis appears in Chapter 5.

Inter-rater reliability

This is usually assessed either by Cohen's kappa, or sometimes more simply by calculating the percentage of times two observers' ratings or categorisations agreed with each other. If there are more than two people making the ratings, Siegel and Castellan (1988) describe a useful non-parametric statistic, Kendall's coefficient of concordance (W).

A note on statistics packages

Many computer statistics packages exist, some of them tailored specifically for the needs of psychologists. The better-known packages exist in forms suitable for Windows. Computer software evolves rapidly and information written now may be out-of-date by the time you read it. Here is a list of different possibilities:

- At the time of writing, SPSS 9.0 and earlier versions of SPSS for Windows have reliability facilities, as well as more standard facilities for factor analysis and the other statistics referred to in this book. Thus SPSS will compute reliability coefficients, item-total correlations, and other statistics relevant to scale construction referred to in this book.
- Older packages offering reliability analysis: the semi-obsolete versions of SPSS (SPSS-X and SPSS-PC), still in use in some parts of the world, CSS/Statistica, and SAS. Detailed guides to the use of these older packages appeared in Loewenthal (1996).
- More modern packages offering reliability include SYSTAT and SAS/STAT.
- Silver and Hittner (1998) describe some software for specialised forms of reliability analysis.
- The CTI web site (p. 163) offers a long list of statistics packages, including a useful search engine. Among the specialist statistics packages accessible through this site, I found QUALPRO, giving inter-coder reliability (which is also available in modern versions of SPSS, but not older ones).

Appendix 5.4 gives instructions for using SPSS to compute reliability.

Validity statistics

Definition of validity and its relation to reliability

A valid test is one that measures what it is supposed to measure. The British Psychological Society (BPS) Steering Committee on Test Standards' *Psychological Testing: A Guide* (1992, p. 6) defines validity as "the relevance of the scores" and the "extent to which it is possible to make appropriate inferences from the test-scores". The 1999 *Guide* says that "validity is concerned with what the test score actually measures" (p. 4). Unless a test is reliable it is unlikely to be valid. There are several different types of validity, and you do not have to use them all. You should select one or more methods, depending on your resources and needs.

Some types of validity

Content and face validity

Content validity is present when the items *are* about what you are measuring, and face validity is present when the items *appear* to be about what you are measuring. Content validity is assessed by asking judges who are experts on the topic being assessed, whether they agree that each item is about what it is supposed to be about. Face validity is normally assessed by asking the same thing of judges who are members of the target population(s) who will be completing the measure. One or more of those who will be administering the test might also be asked. For example "Ice-cream is delicious" is a content- and face-valid measure of favourability to ice-cream, whereas "Ice-lollies are delicious" is not (because ice-lollies are not ice-cream). Some researchers think that face validity is not necessary. There are two reasons for this view. One is that you might see a need to be a bit secretive about what you are assessing, to avoid the possibility of testees "faking-good" (appearing better than they are). Failing to be up-front about what you are measuring will discussed again in Chapters 3 and 4. It raises some serious ethical issues. Another reason for doing without face-validity is that if a test is reliable, and valid by other criteria—it may not matter about face validity. The eminent H.J. Eysenck is reported to have said regarding his measures of neuroticism, "An item can ask whether the moon is made of green cheese, as long as neurotics generally answer one way, and non-neurotics the other." Kline (1986) suggests, however, that participants may not co-operate unless items appear to have face validity. Kline says that if test instructions are clear and all test items reflect all aspects of the subject being tested, then the test is valid *per se*. Jackson (1996) however says that face validity is not a guarantee of other forms of validity, and is therefore not a guarantee that a test is satisfactory for use in a given situation.

Criterion validity

This is present when measures on the test differ as predicted according to some criterion. For example two groups of participants differing by some criterion such as gender, or occupation, might respond differently on many tests.

Concurrent validity

This is shown when your test relates concurrently to some other measure of the same thing. There is always a danger that you can be accused of redundancy, because if you select another test or rating as a criterion against which to validate your test, then you might be asked why your test is necessary at all. You should be able to justify your new measure by showing that it is simpler, quicker, more user-friendly, or more useful or cost-effective than the measure against which you have validated your test. For example, psychometric scales may be more reliable than some traditional methods of assessment, such as interviews, where a great deal of training and experience is required to interpret and score the results.

Predictive validity

This is achieved if your test predicts subsequent performance on some criterion. Occupational psychologists and personnel managers, for example, would normally wish that a selection test would predict future work performance.

Construct validity

This is achieved if you have formulated your test in the context of a theory that makes predictions about behaviour in relation to the test. These predictions would be considerably more elaborate than those expected when looking at criterion or predictive validity. An example would be the predictions made by Eysenck about conditionability and other aspects of behaviour and cognitive functioning according to combinations of scores on the Eysenck personality questionnaire (Eysenck & Eysenck, 1975). Jackson (1996) draws attention to several methods of assessing contruct-related validity. These include *convergent validity*, where there is evidence of similarity of scores on the test, and scores on other tests and measures of the same construct, and *divergent validity*, where scores on the test do not relate to scores on tests or measures of unrelated constructs.

There are other facets to test validity, but the ones I have just described are the types most commonly used. For the novice, and for many ordinary common-or-garden test constructors, it is usually a good idea to try to achieve face and content validity, and usually possible to aim for criterion or concurrent validation against some suitable criterion or standard. Predictive validity sounds straightforward on paper, but it involves a prospective research design—research in which the people tested have to be followed up at a later time. This can be quite difficult in practice— expensive, time-consuming, and often very difficult to track down all the people you tested the first time round—to state the main torments in a nutshell. However it may have to be aimed for when developing a test that will be used for selection and therefore must be shown to predict something (Johnson & Blinkhorn, 1994). As for construct validity, you need a good theory, a lot of courage, and plenty of time and, ideally, research funding. These are things that do not come easily.

The scale

Spell out the scale itself, or sample items, plus instructions to participants. Details of how to go about this appear in Chapter 3. Before you start work, find out if anyone else has already developed a scale measuring what you want to measure. If they have, ensure that you have justified your new measure.

Three more features of most psychological measures

Any measure of the type you might want to construct using this book will involve two important assumptions, namely *additivity* and *interval measurement*.

Additivity

The construct measured (for example, depression, or liking for psychologists) will be assessed by asking people to carry out your instructions with regard to a number of *test items*. You might ask people, for example, whether certain mood-adjectives were generally applicable to them, or whether they agreed with certain statements about psychologists. You then *add up* the answers, to give an overall measure of depression, or liking for psychologists. It is up to you to decide whether *additivity* seems to be justified. It would not make sense to add the answers to depression items to the answers to items about liking for psychologists, for example.

Interval measurement

Once a total score has been obtained by addition, you have to think about whether the "intervals" in your scale are roughly equal. For instance, consider three people scoring say 0, 5, and 10 on a depression measure. To qualify as an interval scale, you have to be fairly confident that the person who scored 10 is more depressed than the person who scored 5, to the *same* extent that the 5-scorer is more depressed than the 0-scorer. If this is difficult to decide, you could comfort yourself with the thought that you may be using Likert's solution, described very shortly. The question of interval scaling is a point dealt with much more fully in statistics textbooks. It is mentioned here because most of the statistics that are needed for scale development assume that scores are on an interval scale. Likert (1932) developed a method for scaling using what he called "equal-*appearing* intervals". This involved asking people to say how *much* they agreed or disagreed with test items, or how much the items were applicable to them. For example, how much do you agree with the following? (Underline one of the five alternative answers.)

"I feel pretty cheerful most of the time." *Strongly agree/agree somewhat/ uncertain/disagree somewhat/strongly disagree.*

Answers to items like this are converted to numbers (+2, +1, 0, −1, −2 for example), and the numbers are added up to give an overall score. The Likert approach is often followed in this book. It should normally be safe to assume that you have at least a rough approximation to an interval scale if you use Likert scaling. Interval measurement is not absolutely essential. For example, yes/no answers are a popular option, and can be used additively. But some answer formats give answers that cannot legitimately be added (for example, ranking in order of preference)—so interval measurement is a good thing to aim for.

Discriminative power

The third important feature of a psychological test is that it should have *discriminative power*. This means that if every person taking the test gets a very similar score—whether all very high, or all very low, or all medium—then the test is useless since it cannot discriminate between people. Such a test will also perform poorly in the statistical evaluation of reliability and validity.

SUMMARY

This chapter stated that the book explains how to construct a reliable, valid measure of reported states of mind or behaviour.

The criteria of "good" psychometric measures were set out, with particular emphasis on reliability and validity. Other important properties include additivity, interval measurement, and discriminatory power.

Chapter 2

A guide to finding and using existing tests and scales

I once heard a delightful remark: "Psychologists would rather use each others' toothbrushes than each others' measures" (Bradley, 1998).

All too true? Very often, it seems that one's research problems cannot be resolved by using any existing measure. None of the measures are quite right. But equally often, it seems that there is duplication of effort in test development. Here, for instance, a historian justly complains about the diversity of measures used by eminent social scientists over a 9-year period, in a series of studies to assess anti-semitism (Dawidowicz, 1977, p. 193):

> Unfortunately, no-one thought to draw up a uniform scale that might be applied to all the surveys . . . *Christian Beliefs and Anti-Semitism* (Glock & Stark, 1966) used six items for its index; *The Apathetic Majority* (Glock, Selznick & Spaeth, 1966), three; *Protest and Prejudice* (Marx, 1967), nine; *The Tenacity of Prejudice* (Selznick & Steinberg, 1969), eleven (seven of Marx's items were the same as Selznick and Steinberg's). *Wayward Shepherds* (Stark, Foster, Glock & Quinley, 1971) changed the ground rules and formulated an index that differed from the one used in *Christian Beliefs and Anti-Semitism* (its predecessor [Glock & Stark, 1996]). The anti-semitism index in *Adolescent Prejudice* (Glock, Wuthnow, Piliavin & Spencer, 1975) consisted of eight items, a few similar to, but none identical with, the eleven-item index in Selznick and Steinberg. Of the various authors, Marx alone employed "positive" items—that is, items favourable toward Jews.

This section describes how to go about discovering whether you are in danger of wasting time by reinventing a psychometric wheel that is already rolling along beautifully. It's better to try to avoid causing complaints like the one just quoted.

FINDING THE SCALE

Here is a list of suggested steps to take to locate an existing measure. If you find something suitable, the later stages in the search can be omitted.

1   Make a note of possible key words covering the content of what you want to assess.
2   Make a note of key features the measure should have, such as type of reliability, type of validity, type of item, etc.
3   Use one or more of the following to identify potential suitable measures:
    • Start with Appendix 2.5, which is a brief review of some popular measures.
    • NFER (National Foundation for Educational Research) Portfolios. Institutions may buy a set of tests that they may photocopy and use freely within the institution. Lists of the measures included in the Mental Health, Health, and Child Psychology Portfolios appear in Appendix 2.3.
    • Try any available stock of measures and tests in your place of work or study.
    • Ask colleagues and acquaintances.
    • Search one or more academic journal databases. The more useful ones are likely to be restricted access: PsychInfo (formerly PsychLit) and the Web of Science (WOS, formerly BIDS) are particularly comprehensive, though even these cover only a minority of academic journals. PsychInfo is the most likely database for discovery of less well-known psychological measures. It gives author, title and publication details, and an abstract, and goes back to the late 1890s. The Web of Science (Social Sciences, going back to the early 1980s) is another possible source. WOS occasionally offers full text versions of articles, in addition to the kind of details outlined for PsychInfo. The simplest way to use PsychInfo or WOS is to ask it to search for the topic(s) and/or author(s) that you want. It will tell you how many abstracts it has found with the word(s) you told it to

look for. If you give it a "big" topic, like depression or memory, there will be too many for you to look through so try to narrow it down by telling it look for, say, depression and chronic and adolescents, or memory and episodic—or whatever your focus is. Ideally you want everything that has been published on your topic without having to wade through too much irrelevant material. When you find something that is on target, make a note of the details and track down the publication in your library, or another library, or via an inter-library loan service. You can print, download, or email the results of your searches for future reference. There is no general public access to services like PsychInfo and WOS. Access must be made through the medium of a university or other subscribing institution. Normally, library services can advise on how to gain access if you are a new user. Some databases *are* freely available on the web, for example Pub-Med (see p. 164), and (for academic books, some of which will contain test and test-related material) Blackwells (see p. 164).

- The ERIC/AE Test Locator (for web site, see p. 163). This supplements the older, hard-copy Buros Institute Mental Measurements Yearbooks (Buros Institute, 1992). Deals generally with published, commercially available tests, and offers detailed reviews of many. There is a search engine, which makes this facility quicker to use than visiting individual publishers' web sites. However, it is not exhaustive.
- Other collections of test reviews and directories include:
  - Maltby, Lewis, and Hill (2000), *A Handbook of Psychological Tests*, which has an excellent web site (see p. 164). This covers recently developed tests (since 1990), covering a full range of psychological factors: cognition, ability, addiction, development, education, occupational psychology, health, well-being, social psychology, personality, and individual differences.
  - Goldman and Mitchell's (1997) *Directory of Unpublished Experimental Mental Measures* covers a range of little-known measures.
  - Bartram, Lindley, Foster, and Marshall's (1990) *Review of Psychometric Tests for Assessment in Vocational Training*, for tests in the occupational psychology area, selection and assessment (see the British

Psychological Society web site for more information and a free leaflet, p. 164).

- Swetland, Keyser, and O'Connor's (1983) *Tests* describes assessments for use in psychology, business, and education, but does not give information on reliability and validity.
- Robinson, Shaver, and Wrightsman's (1991) *Measures of Personality and Social Psychological Attitudes* deals with personality and social psychological attitude measurement.
- Hill and Hood's (1999) *Measures of Religiosity* deals with measures of religiosity.
- Jackson (1996) lists some further collections of test reviews.
- Other hard-copy sources of information, notably Psychological Abstracts, and the Buros Institute Mental Measurements Yearbooks, which have now been replaced by electronic databases described previously, are described more fully in Loewenthal (1996).
- Publishers' catalogues and web sites. A short list of publishers appears in Appendix 2.2. The Buros Institute web site (see p. 163) offers a lengthy list of (mainly US) test publishers. A list of UK publishers is available from the British Psychological Society (see p. 164).
- You may not find everything in the field you are investigating from these sources, as there are a number of smaller-circulation, specialist journals, specialist books, and booklets that have not been covered. Unpublished conference presentations, privately circulated reports, university theses, material used by individuals or research groups are also not covered. You may find something suitable without resorting to these more arcane sources. However, if you need to be thorough, or scholarly, or if you are working in a very specialist field, you may have to use such sources, often involving the setting up of personal links.
- In addition to the web sites specifically given in this book, the general web may be helpful. Try running a few search engines on your search terms.

4   To obtain a *copy* of the test, try:
- Locally available stocks.

- Personal contacts with authors of tests, or others working on the topic you are interested in.
- If available, the NFER (National Foundation for Educational Research) portfolios. Currently these cover Mental Health, Health and Child Psychology, and holders of these portfolios may photocopy the tests (lists of tests are in Appendix 2.3).
- Some published reviews of tests carry copies of the tests, and allow photocopying: for example Hill and Hood (1999) and Robinson et al. (1991).
- Published accounts of tests in academic journals may contain full versions of the tests. These may normally be used, if the author's permission is obtained.
- Commercial test publishers. See Appendix 2.2 for some addresses, and the Buros web site (p. 163) for a much longer list. When buying from a test publisher, remember that you not only have to buy as many copies of the test as you need, but also a test manual and possibly a scoring key. Delivery may take time, especially if the test comes from an overseas distributor. Test publishers operate restrictions concerning who may purchase and use their tests. Buying a test takes time and money. Ensure it assesses what you want it to, and that it meets the requirements of a good test. If you have never seen what the test looks like, you can ask the test distributor for a sample copy before you commit yourself to spending a lot of money.

Key features: Guides on features to look for

The American Psychological Association has produced a very comprehensive list of features (summarised in Appendix 2.1). Briefer guides include the British Psychological Society Steering Committee on Test Standards' very useful booklets, *Psychological Testing: A Guide* (1992, 1999) which outline the features of good psychological measurements and the safeguards to be employed in using them. Another useful booklet is produced by the Institute of Personnel Management (IPM), called the *IPM Code on Psychological Testing* (1993). Appendix 2.1 gives more details.

Copyright

The copyright of published tests is usually owned by the publishers. Anyone who photocopies a test (or who reproduces it by other means) is effectively stealing, and is certainly breaking the law. Some institutions and individuals have been successfully prosecuted for violating copyright, particularly by the use of photocopying. So if a test is published commercially, you may not and should not photocopy it—you should buy it.

Tests published in academic journals may however normally be used, though you should get permission from the author and/or the journal concerned. Academic authors are usually happy to discover that someone is interested in using their test.

Test user restrictions

Some tests require special training: The well-known Rorschach ("ink-blot") test used for describing personality and psychopathology is one example. Another is the Myers-Briggs Type Indicator (Myers & McCaulley, 1985), popular among occupational psychologists, which assesses personality according to the Jungian typology and for which some claims have been made regarding its predictive validity in occupational performance (Ryckman, 1993).

Other tests may not need such specialist training, but professional training and qualifications are required by the test distributors before the test can be obtained. In the UK, Chartered Psychologist status is needed for the use of many tests. A Chartered Psychologist is (briefly) a psychology graduate who has approved postgraduate training and/or qualifications. If you need to find out more details, contact the British Psychological Society (p. 164).

The British Psychological Society awards Certificates of Competence in Occupational Testing (Bartram, 1993; Bartram & Lindley, 2000; British Psychological Society, 1998), further details of which are given in Appendix 2.4. These certificates were originally designed for non-psychologists who need to use psychological tests in their professional work. The BPS is now coming to the view that these certificates should be acquired by psychology graduates, should they wish to do psychometric assessment in occupational settings, since their training in psychometrics may be inadequate.

Some tests may be used under the supervision of a qualified user. Other tests require no special qualifications for use.

Test distributors should and do ensure that tests are purchased only by or for qualified users.

Offensiveness

One final point is that many scales and tests can be seen as threatening, intrusive or offensive by some people, even when there were no apparent problems when they were first developed. For example:

- Some traditional or religious groups of people are particularly likely to find questions to do with sex-related matters offensive. They are not regarded as matter for public discussion or record.
- Many measures of clinical states (perhaps especially depression and anxiety) may be seen as threatening and frightening. I remember one research project in which we were supposed to be using a measure in which the first item was something like "I feel inadequate most of the time". Several participants were alarmed by this, and refused to do the test at all, and we felt very troubled by having tried to use this test.
- There are many other topics that might be very personal or threatening to some people. Likely topics include drug use, suicide, AIDS, and other health problems, finance, religion, and politics.
- Some people may feel that test results reflect on their abilities, or reflect on them in some crucial way. One can never be sure which issues are going to touch an individual most deeply, but you may have a good idea what might be crucial for the kind of people you are going to be testing.

All the safeguards to do with opting-out, anonymity, and other ethical issues described in Chapters 3 and 4 may help to protect people to an extent, but if you have really offended people, these may not be enough. Always be on the look out for the sensitivities of the people you are testing, and be prepared to abandon tests and items that could cause distress, and search for inoffensive ways of examining the constructs you are interested in.

PROS AND CONS OF USING AN EXISTING SCALE

In summary, you might choose to use an existing scale if it:

- can be obtained quickly enough
- can be obtained cheaply enough (preferably free of charge)
- does not require an expensive, time-consuming training
- does not exclude you from using it
- does not contain dated or meaningless language
- measures what you want measured
- is reliable
- is valid
- provides relevant norms
- enables useful comparisons, for example with other groups of people, or with people in conditions different from those you are testing
- does not offend or distress people.

If existing measures "fail" on any of those points, you would be right to develop your own—the biggest loss is probably the opportunity to make meaningful comparisons.

USING THE SCALE

The guidelines to be followed in administering any psychological measure are the same, whether the measure is one you have constructed yourself, or whether the measure was developed by others. The guidelines are described fully in Chapter 4 and in Appendices 2.1 and 4. The main principles are two:

1 Ensure that the sample of people tested is appropriate. Make sure that the people are from groups that you wish to know about, try to ensure that they are a representative sample, and that the numbers are adequate.
2 Ensure that you maintain ethical and legal standards. These include informing yourself about what these are. They range from not violating test user and copyright restrictions, to ensuring that your testing session did not upset anyone, and was a helpful experience for participants.

SUMMARY

This chapter was a guide to finding, choosing, and using existing tests. Resources for locating tests were described, and the criteria to be borne in mind when choosing and using tests were outlined.

Chapter 3

Writing

This chapter describes the first stage of scale development—writing your preliminary scale. This first version will be longer than the final scale. Be prepared to produce more items than you really want to include in the final version. All the items should be as "good" as you can make them at this stage, but some may have to be discarded because they do not meet all the necessary criteria.

DEFINING WHAT YOU WANT TO MEASURE

The first and very important step is to work out and then write down exactly what you want to measure. Show your proposal to all concerned with the work, assess and respond to their comments. You need to be clear about what you are assessing in order to ensure face and content validity. You need to think about whether you are assessing a single psychological factor, or more than one. Often, what seems like a single mood, set of beliefs or other psychological factor, may prove to be more complicated. Examples are:

Anxious mood
Self-rated religiosity
Liking for chocolate
Musical preference.

These all look straightforward, but there are problems with all of them, and similar problems are likely to occur with anything you want to assess. For example:

- With anxious mood, you would need to decide whether you want to distinguish anxiety from depression and other distress states, which may co-occur with anxiety. Otherwise you may finish up assessing forms of distress other than anxiety, without intending to, and finding effects that are not truly the result of "pure" anxiety when you look for performance or behaviour that might be associated with anxiety. You also need to decide whether to define anxiety as the presence of distress states only, or whether you want to look for the absence of positive states such as calmness.

- With religiosity, you would need to decide whether to distinguish between internal religious feelings and experiences, and outward observances, such as affiliation and practice. Are you going to look at one religion or denomination only? Are you going to concern yourself with so-called religious orientation (whether the person claims to be genuinely devout, and/or religious for social or other extrinsic reasons)?

- With liking for chocolate, you would need to think about whether to concern yourself with different forms of chocolate, with the question of chocolate addiction versus liking for the taste, with the roles played by chocolate-eating in the person's life, and so on.

- With musical preference, you would need to decide whether to look at liking for music in general, and different uses of music (listening, performance, therapy, dance, etc.), as well as different types of music.

These are just a few of the kinds of problems. When such problems arise, don't panic! If it all seems straightforward, then something's probably wrong. A group of us were once discussing a research design, and somebody remarked that we seemed to have opened a can of worms and perhaps we should try something more straightforward. My response—endorsed by seasoned colleagues—was that when you are confronted with a can of worms, you can console yourself that you are on the right lines.

The general procedure is to read up what you can about the area of investigation. This will throw up likely problems and hopefully indicate how others have tackled them. You must decide on your own solutions, and be prepared to justify them.

COLLECTING ITEMS

How many items?

Decide approximately how many items you want in your final measure. Too few items may not produce a reliable measure: a notorious feature of the reliability coefficient alpha is that it tends to be low to meet acceptability criteria when there are few items on a scale. If there are too many items, the people you want to test may feel daunted by the length of the scale, and there may be repetitiousness.

Useful scales may contain as few as three or four items, but it is a bit risky to aim for such a short measure. Something between six and fifteen items should be enough for assessing a single "factor". To ensure this, you should start with about 10–30 items. If however you have several subscales, you will need to keep each subscale as short as possible so as not finish up with a monster with 50 or even 100 or more items. No matter how interesting the topic, most people will be fed up before they have finished. As a rough guide, tests with more than one subscale could have about 3–15 items per subscale in the final test, and you need to generate about twice as many for preliminary testing. If you have to have very short subscales, you may wish to try a reliability index other than alpha, or content yourself with low alphas.

Sources of items

Your sources of items will normally be discourse and text. One or more of the following can be used:

- *Brainstorming* sessions—you and others may sit and write items.
- *Conversations*—ideas may be got from this source.
- *Open-ended qualitative interviews*—these are a systematic method of ensuring that you cover the ground than brainstorming or conversation. If you have never done this type of work, you should consult a handbook such as Arksey and Knight (1999), Brenner, Brown, and Canter (1985), or McCracken (1988), or a general research methods handbook with a section on interviewing, such as Breakwell, Hammond, and Fife-Schaw (1994). You will need to construct an interview

schedule—remember that allowing respondents to speak freely is not a free-for-all as far as the investigator is concerned. You will need to ensure that you use listening and prompting skills correctly, and avoid evaluative, over-directive, or interpretive comments—an interview is not a conversation. You should record the methods used to sample or select interviewees, and you need to observe basic research ethics, including confidentiality and making clear to interviewees that they can withdraw at any time.

- *Group discussion (focus group)* sessions. Many of the techniques are similar to those used in interviewing; consult a guide on the use of focus groups such as Higginbotham and Cox (1979), Krueger (1994), or Morgan (1988).
- Published or unpublished *texts* may be used as a source of brief quotes or ideas, which you can use as a basis for your items. With published texts make sure you do not violate copyright restrictions, notably by quoting too heavily from any published work. Quotation of more than about 50 words may need the consent of the copyright holder. With unpublished texts you need to make sure that you are not violating confidentiality.

Checking the items

Having generated or collected a large pool of potential items, items need to be checked to ensure that they meet the following criteria (try to get at least one other opinion as well as your own):

- *Face validity* (see Chapter 6): Does the item appear to be about what you want to assess? For example "I love ice-lollies" has no true face validity on a scale assessing favourability to ice-cream. (You may have decided *not* to aim for face validity.) Face validity should be checked by one or more people from the same population that you are going to ask to complete your measure.
- *Content validity* (see Chapter 6): *Is* the item about what you want to assess? Content validity should be checked by one or more judges who have some expertise in the topic you are assessing.
- *Lack of ambiguity*: "I often feel mad" might be unambiguous to North Americans, but may be ambiguous or misleading to

speakers of British English. Other examples could be quoted. Try to check items with one or more people from the group(s) you are targeting.

- *Not double-barrelled*: It is surprising how often one can finish up with double-barrelled statements, sometimes as a result of trying to achieve clarity; the respondent does not know which "bit" to respond to: for example, "People in authority often do irresponsible or dangerous things".

- *Reverse meaning*: If you are assessing attitudes to or beliefs about a particular issue, it is important to create some items that are "against" the attitude or belief under investigation, to combat the possibility that you may be assessing yea-saying (which is the tendency to agree with any statement, especially if it comes from an authoritative or official-looking source, and which can affect answers quite considerably).

- *Social desirability*: This is something you may not be able to do much about when creating items, but once an item is written, think about whether it might be socially desirable to answer in one way or another; if this possibility exists, you would need to assess social desirability effects. For example, some people may not want to admit to feeling depressed, or angry, or to holding certain beliefs. Alternatively, they may exaggerate the extent to which they feel happy, or hold certain beliefs. A social-desirability measure may be used (e.g., the Marlowe–Crowne Social Desirability Scale; Crowne & Marlowe, 1960). If you are concerned, you may be able set your mind at rest by showing that your measure is not associated with social desirability. If there is an association, you may be able to clean up your measure by weeding-out those items which are strongly associated with social desirability. Or you can use statistical techniques (such as partial correlations) to partial out the effects of social desirability, in any analyses looking at the relations between your measure, and other factors.

- *Offensiveness*: If you are investigating sensitive issues, you need to be particularly careful not to cause offence. Always be alert for this, as you should not be upsetting people—for both ethical *and* pragmatic reasons. If you are concerned about potential threat or offence, first ask members of the group you will be testing (or people who know such members well) whether the items are offensive. Carry out a further check by asking a few people to actually try out the test, and to give their views on possible threat or offence. If a test is offensive or threatening, and you cannot tone it down without losing validity, then you may find less threatening ways (such as face-to-face interviews) of examining the constructs you are interested in. But you may be able to eliminate one or more items without casting aside all of them.

It is very important to get at least one other viewpoint in addition to your own. When you have been closely concerned with creating items, you need a fresh mind to spot most of the previous criteria.

Throw out or re-write until you have items which have face/content validity (assuming that you have no good reason to avoid these forms of validity), which are unambiguous (and not double-barrelled), and unlikely to cause offence. Where appropriate, make sure that some of your items are "reverse-meaning", and think about whether social desirability effects are possible, taking action as suggested previously if necessary.

PRODUCING THE PRELIMINARY QUESTIONNAIRE OR TEST

At last you are ready to produce a preliminary version of the questionnaire or scale. Hopefully you will be word-processing (or, where appropriate, using a graphics package) to produce a nice-looking version. There are a few more points to bear in mind at this stage.

Anonymity, ethics, and the law

There are a number of ethical and legal points to bear in mind when collecting answers to your scale items. Some guidelines from relevant professional and academic organisations appear in Appendix 2.1 and in Appendix 4. The suggestions below should ensure that you do not break any laws or offend anyone. If you are working with special groups such as children, medical patients, disturbed or disabled people then further precautions will have to be taken: These will include getting permission from a research ethics committee who may be helpful about what you need to be careful about. Signed consent may have to be obtained from carers or parents.

Ethically and legally, you may not collect and store information about people in a way that could abuse their trust in giving you information about how they think or feel.

If you are collecting information on one occasion only, anonymity should be guaranteed. Do not, therefore, ask for people's names. It is a good idea to point out explicitly that names should not be written on your forms/questionnaires.

If, however, you want to follow up your participants on a second or subsequent occasion, then you will almost certainly have to identify them, and collect details of how to locate them again. Follow these rules:

1   Identification (name, address, phone number) should be on a separate sheet of paper from other information given by the participant, and should not be entered onto the same database as the research information given by the participants.

2   Make clear to participants that this information will be destroyed as soon as the follow-up is completed.

3   Make sure that you do destroy the information as soon as follow-up is completed.

4   Meanwhile assign each participant a code number, which will enable you to line up the follow-up information with the first lot of information.

5   No cheating: Do not look at the names of who said what, even if the names mean nothing to you. This will protect anonymity if you should ever come across those people again.

As well as guaranteeing anonymity, you need to include a verbal or written assurance that the person giving the information is free to withdraw at any time, and does not need to give reasons for their withdrawal. Some older tests and questionnaires have stern commands such as: "Answer all the questions. Do not leave any out." It is better to avoid this kind of talk. If it is in the *participant's* interest to answer all the questions—for instance if you are trying to get a performance score, or a diagnosis of some kind—you can say something like: "Try to answer all the questions", or "A better/more meaningful result will be obtained if you attempt to answer all the questions." If it is only in the interests of the investigation to get all the answers, then it is better to add an explicit statement such as "If you prefer to omit any question for any reason, please feel free to do so."

Demographic and other data: deciding what is needed

As well as wanting responses to your items, you need to be clear about what other information you need. Decide what you need and work out a format for the information. Background information might include:

age
gender
occupation
religion, etc.

Do not ask for any unnecessary information, and again, be careful not to cause offence.

Response formats

There are several ways in which you might ask for responses to the items in your scale. It is important to use the *same* format for items which are going to be added to each other. If this is not possible you would have to adopt methods of standardisation beyond the scope of this book.

Likert

People are asked to say how *much* they agree/disagree, or how much they think a description applies to them. 5 or 7 points are the most popular. You have a choice about how people are asked to give their response using the Likert format. Figure 3.1 shows one example.

Mark the box which shows how you generally feel

	Strongly agree	Agree somewhat	Neutral	Disagree somewhat	Strongly disagree
It is important to pray when you need help					

Figure 3.1 An example of a Likert-type format

Or, use the formats as in the example in Figure 3.2 (the hypothetical prayer questionnaire), in which people are asked to circle a preferred response, or to write numbers to indicate the extent of agreement/applicability of the statement. (Figure A5.1 in Appendix 5 shows the scoring of this questionnaire.)

Yes/no

A simpler *yes/no* or agree/disagree format may be more suitable in some cases, for example if your scale is part of a survey, and you want to know what percentage of those asked agreed or disagreed with each item. If it is important to get your scale completed quickly, this format can give very rapid completion. You simply instruct people to look through and tick those items they agree with/think apply to them/think are true.

Forced-choice

Another possible format is to ask people to select which of two or more statements or descriptions they prefer or feel is more appropriate. For example:

> Circle A or B, whichever you feel is most true of your feelings:
>
> A   It is important to pray when you need help
> B   Regular contemplative prayer is important.

Appendix 1.1 gives more examples of this forced-choice format. It is a little awkward to score, so make sure you have a good reason for choosing it.

Visual analogue scale (VAS)

This is a horizontal line across the page, on which the person is asked to place a mark to indicate their feelings or beliefs (Figure 5.1 illustrates an example). Responses to these scales are a bit time-consuming to score: You have to measure them. However, some participants like the freedom of being able to place their responses in any position, rather than being forced into categories.

A note on item weighting

In some tests and scales, answers can *weighted*. This is not essential, and if you are a novice, it may be better not to attempt this. Weighting is carried out by multiplying the response to each item by a number that represents the importance of that response in relation to the construct you are measuring. One method of weighting is to carry out a factor analysis and compute a factor score for each item (see Chapter 5). Another, based on Thurstone (1931), is to ask people ("judges") to assign weightings, which are ratings of the relevance or importance of the item to the construct you are assessing, and to take the mean of these. If you suspect that item weighting is needed, consult a more advanced handbook on test construction (such as Anastasi, 1988).

A suggested format

Figure 3.2 shows an example of how the beginning of a questionnaire might look. This example starts with questions on demographic factors (age, gender, etc.), although sometimes it is better to start with the more "interesting" questions of the scale itself. Sometimes however it may be startling or threatening to plunge straight to the point. Only you can decide whether to put the demographic questions before or after the scale.

Set things out so that participants are clear about how to give the information you want, and that they can do this easily.

I prefer to be open about the purposes of any questionnaire or test. This seems the simplest way to maximise the chances of getting honest answers—this, in turn, will improve the psychometric properties of your test (reliability and validity). Some psychologists have suggested that there are occasions when total honesty is not necessarily the best policy. If you feel there are good reasons to practice deception, and conceal the true aims of your questions, then you should bear in mind the need to de-brief participants after they have completed your questionnaire or test. This involves:

- explaining the true purpose of the questionnaire or test;
- explaining why this could not be clear at the beginning;
- offering participants the chance to withdraw the information s/he has given you.

QUESTIONNAIRE ON PRAYER

We are studying people's views on the uses of prayer.
Your answers to the following questions would be very helpful. Your answers will be confidential and anonymous, identified only by a code number. You need not answer any questions that you would prefer to leave unanswered.

Thank you.

Date _____
Your age _____
Male/Female _____
Current marital status (Circle one):
   married
   engaged
   single
   cohabiting
   divorced
   widowed
   separated
Number of children, if any _____
Their ages _____
Your occupation _____
If married or cohabiting, your spouse's occupation _____
Do you regard yourself as spiritual? ─────────
Do you belong to any church, mosque, or synagogue? _____
If yes, which? _____
How often do you attend? (Circle one)
   daily
   weekly
   monthly
   occasionally
   never
How often do you pray? (Circle one)
   daily
   weekly
   monthly
   occasionally
   never
How often do you study religious texts? (Circle one)
   daily
   weekly
   monthly
   occasionally
   never

continues

Write a number next to each of the following statements to show how much you
agree with it:
>   5=strongly agree
>   4=agree somewhat
>   3=uncertain or neutral
>   2=disagree somewhat
>   1=strongly disagree

1 It is important to pray when you need help.
2 There are better routes to understanding life's mysteries than praying.
3 Praying gives comfort.
4 Regular contemplative prayer is important.
5 It is foolish to believe that prayers get answered.
6 People who get inspired by prayer are kidding themselves.
7 Prayer puts things in perspective.
8 Prayer is a waste of time.

Figure 3.2   An example of a simple questionnaire and scale format.

To ensure and demonstrate that you have done this clearly and
consistently, it is a good idea to set the de-briefing out in writing.

Finally, try to set out the questionnaire so as to be as economical
as possible with paper. This saves forests, and photocopying.

SUMMARY

This chapter described the importance of being clear about what
you want to measure, methods of collecting and checking items,
response formats, and the other steps you need to go through to
produce a first questionnaire. Important ethical considerations are
mentioned.

Chapter 4

Testing

Having put together a preliminary questionnaire or test, you are ready to go. The next part is one of the most daunting and also one of the most interesting of the whole process of investigation—finding out what people really think and say in response to your questionnaire.

But—which people?

If you are a student and simply wish to collect as many answers as possible in a short time, then you can run around your college or university begging other students to do your test. But this is not a random sample of anything or anybody, so do not say that it is (some students do!). It is perfectly all right to test students, but when you report your work, say that you used a convenience sample (see later) of students, and give some description of what type of students, and descriptive statistics of at least age and gender.

You may wish or need to test other types of people. If so, here are some points to bear in mind.

DECIDING ON A SAMPLE AND REDUCING SAMPLE BIAS

First, decide what your target population is. You might want as representative sample as possible of British or American or Japanese adults. Or you may be interested in some special group such as women who have just given birth to their first child, professional musicians, adults suffering from a particular anxiety disorder, or users of a particular type of shampoo. You may want to compare people from your target population with one or more comparison groups, who differ from the target group in one or more crucial respects. For example, you might want to compare women who have just given birth to their first child with men who have just become fathers for the first time, or with women with no children, or with women who have just given birth to their second child, or with women with one child who was born say more than 6 months ago—hopefully you know that the idea in comparing two or more groups is to keep all characteristics constant except the one whose effects or correlates you are interested in studying.

In all cases, you decide on a target population, and then select people from it in such as way as to maximise the chances that the people who do your test are as representative as possible of the target population. People who have responded to a call for volunteers are not truly representative, so it is better to try and get a list or source of at least some of the population, sample randomly from that, and approach those selected.

Some methods of sampling are now described.

Methods of sampling

Random and quasi-random

First get a list or source of participants. Any list or source is likely to exclude some of your target population. For example, sampling from a telephone directory excludes those in households with no telephone, the homeless, those who have not yet been listed, and those with ex-directory numbers. Sampling from hospital records to select women who have just given birth to their first child will exclude those who gave birth elsewhere. Try to get the best list you can. You may need to get special permission to get access to the list you need, and hospitals and some other institutions have ethical committees who must approve every piece of proposed investigation to be done on people contacted via the institution. All this can take time and effort to organise, and can sometimes be abortive.

Random sampling means using random numbers to select those to be approached. The random numbers can be computer-generated, taken from a table of random numbers, or you can write numbers on pieces of paper, put them in a container, give them all a good shake and pick out however many you are going to approach. Most books on research methods and statistics have random number tables.

A quasi-random sample involves counting your list and taking one name in every five (or ten, or whatever). Unless you suspect that this will produce a systematic bias, this method can be used if you want something a bit simpler than true random sampling.

If you are you using random or quasi-random sampling you will need to decide what to do, if you cannot contact the person identified by the sampling strategy, or if the person you have identified refuses to participate. One common practice is to make three attempts to contact the targeted person. If no success after three attempts, or if a person declines to participate, you could replace them with the next name on the list.

Quota/target group

Sometimes you can try to achieve representativeness by taking quotas of people from particular categories, in the proportions in which they are reported to occur in that population (or in the proportions that you need for your research design). For example, you might take equal numbers of men and women, and equal numbers of socio-economic groups ABC1 and C2DE. This is sometimes called stratified sampling, and it can be done randomly within quotas.

However, where you are simply aiming to fill a quota, or to recruit a certain number from a target group, you are not committed to random sampling. You are more likely to get sample bias if you do not use random sampling, but if you are interested in looking at differences between two groups in relation to some independent or classification variable (gender, occupation, use of particular types of shampoo, and so forth) this may not really matter so much (see later for possible methods). You should, however, try to ensure that your quotas or target groups have been equated for factors that may affect what you are assessing, such as age, general health, intellectual functioning, and so forth.

Convenience and snowball

These are two non-random methods, which may be used to fill quotas or target groups. There are other methods (see for example Coolican, 1999) but these are the two most straightforward.

Convenience sampling means testing whoever it is convenient to test. Sometimes this is called opportunity sampling. Sample bias is more likely than if random methods are used, but as I said earlier, if you interested in the effects or correlates of a particular independent variable, then random sampling may be less important than if you wanted to find out the general level of response to your questions. For example if you were investigating fear of death or liking for ice-cream, you would try to get a random sample from the general population if you were interested in "absolute" levels of—or proportions of people with—fear of death or liking for ice-cream. If, however, you were interested in the effects of a particular religious belief on fear of death, or of hot weather on liking for ice-cream, then random sampling does not matter so much because you are looking at *relative* levels—for example, whether stronger belief in life after death is associated with *lower* levels of fear of death, or whether hot weather is associated with *higher* levels of liking for ice-cream than is cold weather. As I said before, you obviously need to consider whether the independent variable you are looking at (belief in life after death, hot weather) may be confounded with other variables. Especially if you are using convenience sampling, keep a watchful eye on factors, like age, which might affect what you are assessing. Try to ensure that your groups are comparable on such variables (or use appropriate statistics, as described in Chapter 6 and Appendix 6.5, for "partialling-out" the unwanted effects of confounded variables).

Snowball sampling is useful when you want to fill quotas or target groups, and there is no ready supply of suitable people underfoot. You might want to locate people with a particular (but rare) disability, or set of beliefs, or a particular ethnic group. You locate one suitable person who is willing to do your test, and ask them if they can suggest one or two others who might be willing to help, and then those people are asked for more names, and so on. In the shampoo-user case, you might ask if the person knows whether any of their friends use this type of shampoo. This method of recruitment is pleasant to use, because there is less ice to break. You may already have an "introduction"; you can ask the person giving you each name whether they mind their name being mentioned when you approach their acquaintance. Usually it is very effective. Of course it does not give a random sample.

More detailed discussions of sampling methodology may be found for example in Coolican (1999), De Vaus (1993), or Kish (1965).

Response rates

If you are trying to ensure minimum sample bias, then you have to be able to demonstrate that no bias was introduced at the stage of recruitment by large numbers of people declining to do your questionnaire. Keep a record of:

1 How many people could not be contacted (for example you wrote to them and they did not reply; then you tried phoning, say three times, but there was no answer—or someone answered the phone, but not the person you were seeking, of whom they have never heard);

2 How many people you contacted but who declined to participate (Y);

3 How many people you contacted and who agreed to participate (X); if they started but did not finish, you can still count them as participants—unless they said they wanted their record destroyed. Missing answers can be entered as missing values on the computer, and you will still have some usable data from those people who did something but did not complete.

To calculate response rate, you could normally disregard category 1. Response rate is the percent of participants, out of the total number of people who were asked to participate, i.e.:

Response rate = $[(X/(X+Y) \times 100]\%$.
(Where "Y" and "X" are the numbers of people recorded under categories 2 and 3.)

Published research usually reports response rates of at least 70%, with rates well over 90% in many investigations. Occasionally there may be special groups or other circumstances involving low response rates of the order of 50% or less. Low response rates are common in postal surveys. When rates are below about 70% you have to consider whether there is any sample bias among those agreeing to participate. This can be difficult, of course, because it could be difficult to find out anything about people who could not or would not answer any of your questions. But you can look for over-representation of certain groups of people among those who did participate. You might find, for instance, that there are more retired or unemployed people in your sample than you might expect from what is known about the proportions of these groups in the population you are studying.

When reporting your findings, report response rates, and, if they were low, say what you can about how the sample appeared to be biased and how this might have affected responses to your questionnaire or test.

Sample size and statistical power

It is often thought good to aim for large samples. This is not always so (Coolican, 1999) since averaging what large numbers of people have said or done may conceal important individual or group differences. The two principal reasons for trying to get a large sample are:

- *Reduced sample bias*: Sample bias is generally reduced in larger samples.
- *Improved statistical power*: If you are looking for statistically significant differences or associations, the power of the statistical test to detect such differences is related to sample size. Statistical power is also related to the size of the effects you have got (or hope to get), and to what you have decided is an acceptable level of statistical significance. Cohen (1988) explains all, and Cohen (1992) explains all you probably need to know for most purposes. Statistical power is stated by Cohen (1992) to be the probability that a given investigation will lead to statistically significant results. This latter very helpful guide explains that normally a power specification of 0.80 would be made, and one would normally expect a medium effect size; if then alpha (acceptable significance level) is set at .05, Table 4.1 shows the minimum sample sizes required (note that in the context of discussions of statistical power, "alpha" has nothing to do with the reliability coefficient of that name). This brief description of statistical power probably needs to be supplemented by referring to Cohen (1992). But even if you read no further on this topic, Table 4.1 suggests minimum sample sizes for some common research scenarios, so that the researcher can be reasonably confident that if no significant effect was detected, this was not simply because the sample size was too small.

Table 4.1 Minimum sample sizes for some basic
research designs (adapted from Cohen, 1992)

Test	Minimum sample size	
	Group	*Total*
Mean difference (*t* test)	64	128
Correlation		85
X^2 with 1 *df*		87
Anova with 3 groups	52	156
Anova with 4 groups	45	180

The sample sizes given apply where a medium effect size is expected, alpha
is .05, and the power specification is 0.80.

You would need to consult Cohen (1988 or 1992) for required
sample sizes where effect size and alpha differ from those described
above, and for further research designs and statistical tests. The
figures in Table 4.1 are for some common scenarios. Brewin
(personal communication in 1993) has pointed out that if the
principles of power analysis are applied—and there are increasing
calls for this to be done—then the trend should be towards simpler
research designs, with smaller numbers of groups (and independent
variables), in order to ensure adequate sample sizes.

As Table 4.1 indicates, samples of hundreds and thousands are
not essential. Sample size should give adequate statistical power to
detect the effects you are interested in, and should be sufficient for
you to be reasonably confident that bias is unlikely.

RECRUITING METHODS

You now have to persuade people to do your questionnaire or test.
Some suggested methods are described next.

Direct approach

This involves a direct approach! You approach a potential participant saying something along the following lines: "Good morning/
afternoon. My name is . . ., and I am (a student at . . ./working for
. . . . I/we are conducting a study of (topic) and I/we would be very
grateful if you spare a few minutes to (answer a few questions/look
at this questionnaire and see if you would be willing to answer the

questions)." People may be approached by door-to-door calling (carry some identification and credentials) or in the street, provided you choose a safe area and time of day. If you are a student, your campus is probably safest.

Mail

Mail shots produce notoriously poor response rates (normally well under 50%).

Telephone

Some researchers call telephoning a stranger out of the blue "cold-calling", and this may also yield a poor response rate. A good combination is to send a letter explaining the purpose of your investigation, and explaining that you are going to telephone shortly to ask if the person is willing to help. When you phone, remind the person that you wrote about the research, and if they do not seem to be aware of this, briefly summarise the contents of the letter. Normally, most people will recall your letter, and you will have saved yourself a lot of time explaining the basics, and if the answer is to be a "no", at least it is usually given quickly.

Use of institutions

It is always tempting to consider this, since you may have access to large numbers of the type of people you are looking for, and it may even be possible to test groups of people together. However institutions must protect their members, and you will usually have to get through a lot of red tape before you get permission to approach people through institutions. Some (especially hospitals and other health service institutions) will have their own ethical committees. Be prepared to submit a written proposal, explaining and justifying your research and explaining why you need to approach people through the institution. You will also need to submit a copy of your questionnaire, and explain who you are, and you may have to meet one or more bosses. Be prepared for a long wait—sometimes several months—and a possible rejection. Do not, therefore, rely on one institution. If you have "contacts", this can be useful, as personal acquaintance may reassure those responsible that you can (hopefully) be trusted, that you are doing something useful, and will behave responsibly. If your work will produce something that is useful to the institution, that is an advantage.

Ethical issues

The most important underlying principle is respect—respect for the right to choose to help, respect for privacy, respect for confidentiality. It is also important to express *thanks* for help, and to *explain* how the help that has been given will be used and will be useful.

Opting-out and opting-in

People recruited to do your questionnaire or test should always be invited (not coerced) to participate, and it should always be made clear that they should omit any question they prefer not to answer, and are free to stop at any time *without giving a reason* (opting-out). Some ethical committees may require participants to sign a consent form agreeing to participate (opting-in). This is more commonly needed in medical than in psychological research. Opting-in can produce a lowered response rate, but may be an important safeguard when researching sensitive topics, or special groups of people.

An important set of safeguards is that you should make sure that testing conditions are *private* (ensure that the participant's answers cannot be overseen or overheard) and undisturbed, and that participants know that their answers are to be treated *confidentially and anonymously*.

Feedback may be given (see later). Consult the guidelines in Appendix 4.3.

Appendices 2.1 and 4 offer other ethical considerations and further suggestions about how to put ethical principles into practice.

TESTING

Decide whether you want people to write their answers, or deliver them verbally. You may in some circumstances want to use computerised testing. Writing (or computer) is a more efficient way of collecting responses from literate adults than speaking, and where there are no obvious difficulties. Remember to provide necessary writing instruments, a firm surface to write on, and private, quiet, undisturbed surroundings.

If, however, you have a short questionnaire, which you are delivering "on the trot", or if you are testing children, or adults who might have some difficulty with reading or writing, then you need to collect spoken answers. Short answers can be written down, but if you have any open-ended questions you may need to use a tape-recorder. Some people do not like this, and you obviously need to get their permission to record. Make sure you promise to turn the machine off the minute they ask for this. You can also reassure people that they will probably stop noticing the recorder after a couple of minutes.

Sometimes there might be good reason to record speech or behaviour—whether in writing or otherwise—*without the person's awareness*, for example in making naturalistic observations of speech or behaviour, in say shopping, waiting for a medical consultation, or crossing the street. This is not very likely in normal questionnaire and assessment work, but it might arise with a very short measure in which a very few questions had to be asked face-to-face. Make sure that the "victim" knows what you have done, and has given permission for you to use your records of what they have said or done.

Appendix 4 offers further guidelines on testing and feedback.

Group or individual testing?

Groups of people are often hard to come by, but testing groups usually yields results more quickly than testing individuals. You should try to make sure that everyone has understood the instructions, and is feeling happy about co-operating. If you fail on either point, you may get too many spoilt questionnaires, and if they are completely spoilt you will have to record them as non-responses rather than incomplete.

With a group, it is a good idea to stress that opting-out is always possible, and to provide opportunities for those who wish to leave the room, or to engage in alternative activities, to do so. Finally, it is important to make sure that conditions are such that people can complete the test or questionnaire in privacy, without disturbance from others in the room.

Thanking, debriefing, and follow-up

Remember to thank your respondents, and to add any further explanations about the work that are necessary. Answer all questions as well as you can. You can offer to send results for those who are interested. In this case, participants will have to leave their names and addresses. Make sure this information is stored separately from responses to questionnaires, in order to protect anonymity. You can send either a copy of your report provided it is not too technical, or confidential, or a summary of your results prepared especially for participants. Do not forget to add a note of thanks for their help, and give your name and address in case further questions arise. In some cases it may be appropriate to offer individual feedback. This should always be done privately, and never in a critical or damaging way.

SUMMARY

This chapter described the things you need to be careful about in selecting and approaching participants, in order to ensure a sample which is as representative as possible of the group(s) tested. The chapter also describes means of protecting the well-being of the people participating in the development of your measure.

Chapter 5

Data and preliminary analysis

Having got your questionnaires and tests completed by as many people as you need, you can now enter the data onto a computer database, coding the information where necessary, and ensuring that the records of each person are not named. Then you will work out which are the best, most reliable, items in your scale and discard the rest. You will then have a "final" scale consisting of these reliable items, on which you can work out a final total for each participant, and produce descriptive statistics for this final scale (norms). This final scale will then be ready for validation work.

For each stage I will describe what has to be done, and a general explanation of how to do it. Appendix 5.3 gives examples of how to do it in SPSS.

CODING, SCORING, AND DATA ENTRY

Coding

Responses that do not need coding

1   Most answers that are already in numerical form, such as *age*, and the *answers to scale items*, if these were given in a numerical form, for example +2, +1, 0, −1, −2, or 5, 4, 3, 2, 1. You do not need to do anything except enter them as they are onto the computer database.
2   Answers with a *yes/no* response format can also be entered directly onto the computer database: 1 for a "yes" and 0 for a "no".

Table 5.1　Examples of items that do not need coding

Type of item	Example	Example of answer	What you enter on database
Item requiring numerical answer	Age	23	23
Likert-type scale item	Liking for this chocolate (1=very low, 2=quite low, 3=moderate, 4=quite high, 5=very high)	4	4
Yes/no or checklist	Mark words that apply to this chocolate:		
	sweet	×	1
	creamy	×	1
	bitter		0
	spicy		0
Forced-choice	Which one would you choose for your next snack:		
	this chocolate	×	1
	another chocolate		0
	another snack		0

3 If you were using a *checklist* format, answers to each item would be entered as 1 where an item had been checked, and 0 where it had not, with a new column in the database for each item. Strictly speaking, this *is* coding, but it is so simple that you can enter the coded responses straight onto the computer database.

4 *Forced-choice* format answers, where your participants have to select one of several alternatives: You can enter 1 for items selected, and 0 for those not selected. Later, you can compute scores from this information.

Table 5.1 shows examples of answers that do not need coding and which can be entered directly onto the computer database. If no answer has been given, leave the corresponding space in the database blank, to indicate missing data. There is no need to enter anything special to represent missing information, even though this used to be necessary for older statistics packages. Alphabetical

information needs special treatment beyond the scope of this book. Therefore, as just indicated, translate "yes" into "1", and "no" into "0".

Information that needs coding

Other information will need to be coded so that you can do statistics. To speed things up and reduce errors, many researchers pre-code their questionnaires by placing the appropriate code next to each response option. For example:

How much do you like this chocolate? (tick one answer)		(Office use only)
VERY MUCH	□	5
QUITE A LOT	□	4
MODERATELY	□	3
NOT VERY MUCH	□	2
NOT AT ALL	□	1

The codes are put in an out-of-the-way column, perhaps with that useful heading "Office use only".

Types of information that need coding are:

1   If your participants answered your scale items by checking one of several ordered responses, instead of writing a number: for example "strongly agree, agree somewhat, neutral, disagree somewhat or strongly disagree". In such a case you simply translate the answers into a simple ordered number scale. In this case, it could be +2, +1, 0, –1, –2, or 5, 4, 3, 2, 1. It does not matter which, as long as you *consistently* apply the *same* scale to *each* item. You can use this procedure for a scale with any number of points: 3, 5, 7, 9, and 11 are the most common. You might wonder what to do about "*reverse-meaning*" items, where agreeing with such items suggests an "opposite" set of beliefs or attitudes or feelings, compared to agreeing with other items. In such cases, you still give the same "score" to "strongly

On each line, place a mark to indicate how this chocolate tastes:

For example, if you think the chocolate tastes very pleasant, put a mark very near the word pleasant, like this:

Pleasant x_____ Unpleasant

If you think the chocolate is quite unpleasant, place a mark quite near the word unpleasant:

Pleasant _____x___ Unpleasant

If you think the chocolate is neither pleasant nor unpleasant, put a mark near the middle:

Pleasant _____x_____ Unpleasant

Mark each line to show what you thought of the chocolate:
Sweet _x_____ Bitter
Boring _____x_____ Exciting
Sharp _____x Creamy
Bland ____x_____ Tasty

Figure 5.1 Visual analogue scales (VASs), with instructions.

agree" and so forth. However, later, you will have to tell the computer to *reverse* the scoring of such items. Appendix 5 offers instructions.

2   A *visual analogue scale* (VAS) is a horizontal line across the page, on which the person is asked to place a mark to indicate their feelings or beliefs. Figure 5.1 shows an example. As stated in Chapter 3, responses to these scales are more time-consuming to score than other types of response, so consider whether it is worthwhile to use this method. The example suggests that the person tested perceived the chocolate as sweet and creamy, bland and rather boring. With a VAS, you score the answers by measuring the distance in centimetres or millimetres from the left-hand end of the line. This number is entered onto the database. When describing variables assessed on a VAS, use the word on the *right*-hand side of the scale. If necessary, reverse the scoring (by subtraction) once all the data are entered in the database.

3   If you have asked for background socio-demographic data from your participants, some of these (such as gender, occupation, or group membership) will need to be translated into an appropriate number scale. You should be aware of what *type of*

number scale (interval, ordinal, or categorical) you are using because this will affect the kind of statistics that are appropriate. Consult Appendices 5.1 and 5.2 if you feel doubtful.

When to calculate total scores

If you are using a computer, there is normally no point in calculating people's total scores on the scale by hand. Assuming you are going to do a reliability analysis, the computer software will calculate the totals it needs. Following reliability analysis, you will discard some of the items on the scale, and then you will be able to calculate total scores on your refined scale. You will be able to do this using the computer.

However, it is a good idea to reverse the scoring of any "reverse-meaning" items as soon as possible after entering all the data, and to save these reversed scores. This chapter and Appendix 5 describe how to do this.

So, total scores on the scale are not computed until *after* the data are entered, reverse-meaning item scores are reversed, reliability has been investigated, and non-cohesive items have been discarded.

Make a database

This can be done using SPSS, or other statistics package. If necessary, in the absence of a statistics package spreadsheet, a modern word-processing or spreadsheet package could be used. But you will eventually have to import the data into a statistics package for processing. If you are making the database using software which is different from the one you will be using for statistics, make sure that your statistics package can use the database, or that you can translate the database into a form that can be used by your statistics package. SPSS for Windows, for example, will be able to import Excel, text, and ASCII files, as well as system files made for pre-Windows versions of SPSS. However, with text and ASCII files you will have to work hard at defining the variables. It is very much better to enter your data into the spreadsheet of the statistics package you will be using.

To enter data:

• Start with an ID number for each participant (person that did your test). This will be the first column on the spreadsheet.

- Name all the remaining columns with the variable names, such as age, gender, item1, item2, etc. If wished, you can take the opportunity to define what each code number represents, for example 0 = male, 1 = female.
- Enter the coded responses to your questions, including the answers to the main part of the questionnaire, which can be entered just as they are, if they are in numerical form. Data should normally be in numerical form—seek advice if you think you have to enter alphabetical information.
- Make sure you start a new line/row for each participant.
- Make sure that you have the right number of pieces of data for each participant. Thus each line of data should finish in the column of the last variable. This sounds obvious, but if you are doing a lot of data entry, or if (like me) you are inclined to rush and make mistakes, you can find that you have entered all the data for one participant, but you are a column too early or a column too late. This means that you will have to go back and check until you find where the error was made.
- If any answer is missing, leave the space in the spreadsheet blank. (Only if you are word-processing, will you need to assign a number for all *missing values*. Decide on a number that is not otherwise going to be used (–1, 9, and 99 are popular for missing values), and put that whenever an answer is missing).

If you get stuck, consult Cramer (1993), Field (2000), Foster (1993) or any other book on SPSS or computing for social scientists or psychologists, or ask a friend with relevant computing experience, or a computing adviser.

Remember to *save* the database as you go along, especially if you have a big database. Also, make a back-up copy on a floppy disc and/or file server. Normally you would continue to use the same filename each time you save, over-writing the older version.

Check for accuracy

Once the database is complete, you should carry out one or more checks for accuracy, before you can start statistical analyses. Appendix 5.3 discusses the procedures outlined here in more detail.

- Scan the database for numbers that should not be there. For example a common "typo" in data entry is of the type "25", where you should have typed "2" and "5" in adjacent cells.
- If you are using a statistics package, ask for frequencies of variables and scan the results. When you scan, look for unlikely or impossible values, such as "2" or "99" on age, in a study where you know that all participants were aged 18–65, or "0", "6", or "25" on a scale with a range of 1–5. Locate any error on the database, find the true value, and enter it.
- Finally, if possible, carry out a check on the print-out of the database. This easiest if working in pairs. One member of each pair looks at the original data, and the other looks at the database. One person reads out the data. It doesn't matter which person—take turns. The other person calls out when they spot a mis-match. Correct all mistakes on the computer database, and save the corrected version.

Reverse scoring and saving the database

You can now

- *recode* any negatively-worded (reverse-meaning) items,
- deal with missing values, if necessary (see the end of Appendix 5.3 for details),
- *save and back up your data file.*

Appendix 5.3 provides instructions for doing this using SPSS for Windows.

SELECTING RELIABLE ITEMS

Instructions for computing reliability appear in Appendix 5.4.

The first reliability statistics

Chapter 1 defined the main types of reliability. SPSS or other statistics package with a reliability facility (Chapter 1 lists some packages) will normally give you one reliability statistic (Cronbach's alpha) by default, and you can specify others if needed. There are ways of examining reliability without a reliability facility, or even without a statistics package. In the (hopefully) unlikely event of such a need arising, Loewenthal (1996) describes how this can be done.

If you want to understand more fully what the different reliability options mean, Chapter 1 gives an outline. You should also study the statistics package handbook, combined with a handbook of test construction such as Anastasi and Urbina (1996) or Kline (1999).

The first reliability statistic to look at is Cronbach's alpha, a widely used reliability coefficient. This is normally sufficient. This is the estimated correlation of the test with any other test of the same length with similar items (i.e., items from the same item universe). The square root of alpha is the estimated correlation of the test with true scores.

What are the *criteria of acceptability for reliability coefficients*? Kline (1993) recommends a minimum of 0.80. The British Psychological Society Steering Committee on Test Standards (1995) suggests that 0.70 might be acceptable. If you have a scale with a small number of items, you are not likely to get reliability coefficients as high as this, and you may consider using a slightly lower criteria (of about 0.6) *if* (and only if):

- there is good evidence for validity,
- there are good theoretical and/or practical reasons for the scale, and
- the scale is short (less than about 10 items).

Some test constructors develop tests that are long and repetitive. These features are likely to ensure high reliability coefficients. However it is *not* very good practice to write tests in this way. Participants may get bored or suspicious if the same sort of question is asked over and over again, and improving internal consistency by these dubious means will not improve validity. It is better to settle for an alpha of around 0.60, given the conditions listed previously.

However, there are legitimate steps you can take to improve the reliability of your scale. The first thing to try is "cleaning up" your scale by weeding-out those items that are lowering the internal cohesiveness. The next subsection ("Improving the reliability of the scale") describes how this can be done.

The K-R 20 (Kuder-Richardson 20) is a special case of the alpha coefficient, for items that have been dichotomously scored. You should not have to do anything to get this statistic. Your reliability facility should produce it automatically when there are only two values on a variable, instead of Cronbach's alpha. It can be interpreted in the same way.

Your reliability facility can compute other reliability coefficients (split-half, for example—see your menus or handbook for the full range of possibilities), but normally Cronbach's alpha, probably the default option, should be used. This is regarded by Cronbach (1951) and Nunnally (1978) as the most important index of test reliability. The split-half reliability coefficient could be useful if you have only a small number of items in a scale or subscale, since in this situation you may not get a sufficiently high alpha.

If you think there might be some subscales within your overall scale, you can get alphas for the subscales, by computing alphas for just those items comprising each subscale. For instance, in our prayer example in Figure 3.2 the scale was written with two kinds of items: those valuing prayer as a way of getting what one wants (instrumental), and those looking at prayer as a form of strengthening or inspiring communication with the divine (inspirational). You could look at the reliabilities of subscales like these. Appendix 5.5 gives instructions for computing and improving reliability of scales, and exactly the same procedures are followed for any subscales.

If your test/scale used a *forced-choice* format, you may need to compute the reliabilities of the different subscales covered by the choices offered to the participants. For example, if you wanted to find out people's habitual distress mode, you might present a number of items like this:

"When someone pushes in front of me on line, I feel on the whole:
  angry
  tense
  worthless."

"When I get disappointing news, such as doing worse than expected in a test, I feel on the whole:
  depressed
  worried
  annoyed."

In this example, people are asked to choose *one* answer. There are three hypothetical subscales (anger, depression, and anxiety) and the score on each is the number of times a relevant emotion is chosen. You would need to look at reliabilities for all three subscales. However, if your forced-choice alternatives are just "rubbish" apart from the one you are interested in, there is obviously no need to look at subscale reliabilities. For example, in tests of knowledge or ability, the alternatives to the correct answer do not form separate subscales, as in:

"Churchill was:

a World War II General

a British Prime Minister

the place of a famous battle."

"Pearl Harbour was:

the place of a famous battle

a singer

a jewellery shop."

The score here is the number of correct items endorsed and, since there is no rhyme or reason in the alternatives, you do not treat them as subscales.

Improving the reliability of the scale

There are five courses of action, and if you are lucky you may not have to follow these through past number one or two. If you are very unlucky, you will have to work your way through all five.

1   You may have high reliability coefficients, and might decide to keep your scale (and any subscales) as it stands. No action is needed.
2   If your reliabilities are low, you must look at each item to see how it relates to all the others. This is worth doing even with high reliability if you want to improve the reliability still further. This is done by looking at item-total correlations. A reliability facility can give item-total correlations between each

item and the total of the *other* items in the scale. Thus the total is not contaminated by the contribution of the item in question. This indexes the *cohesiveness* of the scale. Loewenthal (1996) suggests how to examine scale cohesiveness without a reliability facility.

If you have subscales you should look at correlations between each item from each subscale with the relevant subscale totals in exactly the same way as for the overall scale, simply using the items involved in the subscale.

You reject items with unsatisfactory item-total correlations.

Your reliability facility will probably tell you *the effect on the reliability coefficient of removing any given item*. This information will tell a similar story to the item-total correlation, and you may find it simpler and clearer to go straight for this information as a way of improving your scale. You can overlook the item-total correlations, or glance at them to check that they confirm that you have made the right decisions. Items with *low* item-total correlations should be the ones whose removal leads to the *biggest* improvement in the reliability coefficient.

3   If the number of items in your scale (or subscale) is small, alpha is likely to be low even if they are quite strongly associated with each other. Try calculating split-half reliability, which involves the following steps:

- divide the items randomly into two groups of equal size,
- calculate a total for each of these half-scales,
- calculate the correlation coefficient between these half-scales.

Note that a reliability facility will normally do the calculations for you without you personally having to go through the separate steps.

4   A scale may have poor overall cohesiveness, and this may be because there are subscales (factors) that you had not suspected. Try factor, or principal components analysis (see the section on this topic later in this chapter). If the results make sense and produce a factor (or factors) on which items with high loadings relate to the construct(s) you are assessing, then items with high loadings (0.3 or 0.4 and above) are retained.

Note that this method may give you two or more factors, suggesting the existence of two or more subscales. For each subscale, retain and score only those items with high loadings on the relevant factor. Note that if an item has a negative loading, its score will have to be reversed.

Strictly speaking, if you have identified two or more subscales using factor or principal components analysis, you do not need to confirm this by doing a reliability analysis of the subscales.

5   The last and saddest resort is to salvage any items that seem worthwhile, write some more items, and start testing again. However, as discussed, avoid the all-too-common failing of generating a lot of repetitious items.

DESCRIPTIVE STATISTICS (NORMS) FOR THE FINAL SCALE

You define your final scale by listing only those items with satisfactory item-total correlation, and obtain Cronbach's alpha (or other reliability coefficient), the number of cases, mean, range and variance of the final scale, and of any subscales.

Some would prefer to divide the scale mean by the number of items in the scale, to give an *item mean*. The advantage of this is that if the number of items in the scale is ever changed at a later date, then comparisons involving the item mean would still make some sense.

If you have decided to use *item weightings*, then answers to each item must be multiplied by the relevant weighting before the mean score on the scale is determined.

The production of *standardised scores* is beyond the scope of this book, and Anastasi (1988) or Kline (1999) should be followed if these are desired.

SUMMARY OF STEPS FOR DATA ENTRY AND RELIABILITY

1   Code data where needed.
2   Enter data.
3   Check data.

4   Recode where necessary (for "reverse-meaning" items).
5   Save data file, making at least one back-up copy.
6   Compute the reliability coefficient (usually Cronbach's alpha) for the scale, and for any subscales. If satisfactory, you can go straight to step 9.
7   If this is unsatisfactory (less than 0.70–0.80) examine item-total correlations (scale cohesiveness).
8   Remove items with unsatisfactory item-total correlations.
9   Produce total scores and descriptive statistics (norms) for the final scale, containing only those items with satisfactory item-total correlations: number of cases, mean, range and variance (or standard deviation), and reliability coefficients.

If this fails to produce a scale with a satisfactory reliability coefficient, you could attempt a factor (principal components) analysis, as described in the next section and in Appendix 5.6.

If ever describing any scale with dubious reliability, you should state clearly that the scale does not meet criteria for reliability.

FACTOR AND PRINCIPAL COMPONENTS ANALYSES

If you are developing a scale for professional use or major research purposes, some psychometricians would regard factor analysis as an important, or even essential procedure in the construction of psychological scales and tests. If, however, you have obtained satisfactory reliability and/or you are not applying the scale in a major way, you could skip this bit. As discussed earlier in this chapter, you might consider this analysis as a way of identifying possible subscales, if your measure has poor internal consistency.

The underlying theory is a specialist aspect of statistics, and there is a good deal of controversy surrounding the applications of factor analysis. Chapter 1 refers to relevant discussions.

For those taking first steps in scale construction, you could consider using factor analysis if you thought there were several factors in your scale, but you were not sure which items were contributing to them. Factor analysis will tell you the answers to these questions, and so, too will principal components analysis. Chapter 1 gives a brief description of factor and principal components analyses and explains the difference between them. It is suggested that principal components analysis may give clearer answers than factor analysis. Appendix 5.6. offers brief instructions for carrying out factor/principal components analysis.

If you do a factor analysis, you need to examine which items load heavily on each factor. Common criteria are:

- normally, loadings of 0.4 and above, or
- loadings of 0.3 and above where there are few or no high loadings, for example, and where it would make sense in naming the factors to include items with slightly lower loadings.

Name the factor according to the items that load heavily on it. To do this, make a list of high-loading items, and look for a common feature. Note that *negative* loadings indicate that the item is negatively associated with the factor.

You do not have to accept and use all the factors. A rough guide to deciding which factors to accept is as follows:

- The first 1–4 factors will probably account for quite a lot of variance each, and after that there may be a sudden drop. A likely type of scenario would be for factor 1 to account for about 13%, factor 2 about 8%, and then factors 3 and 4 to account only for a mere 3% or 4% each. Look for such a drop, and use it as a cut-off point in accepting which factors to use. Modern versions of SPSS will normally drop factors which account for insufficient variance.
- Only accept factors accounting for, say, about 8% or more of the variance. Thus in this example, only consider using factors 1 and 2.
- Only accept factors that make sense in terms of the constructs you are assessing. Of course, a reasonable amount of variance should be accounted for. This means that if a factor accounts for a lot of variance, and it does not make sense or is not of interest to you—then you don't have to use it!

If you do a factor analysis you may want to consider whether to use *item weightings*. Weighting the items means that an item with high weighting contributes more to the score than an item with low weighting. The main advantage of weighting is that it could give a more sensitive scale, possibly with improved validity. The main disadvantage is that calculation of scale totals and norming data is more complicated and time-consuming. Responses to each item have to multiplied by the item weighting (of course this is normally done by the computer). You could certainly consider using weighted scores if you find the results of your validity analyses are disappointing. There are several ways of developing item weightings: Factor loadings can be used as item weightings, or the factor analysis facility on a statistics package will calculate factor scores. Consult your statistics package manual if necessary. If you are thinking of using item weightings, a more advanced manual on test construction should be consulted.

A simpler application of factor analysis, which has some of the advantages of item weighting without the disadvantages, is to *use the factor loadings as criteria* for retaining items in the scale(s). Decide whether to use a loading of 0.3 or 0.4 as a cut-off, and accept only items with this loading or higher in your scale(s). This may improve the sensitivity and reliability of your scale, without the extra computational labour of item weightings. However unless you had an undiscovered subscale structure embedded in your scale, which only factor analysis could reveal, this method is unlikely to give better results than a reliability (item) analysis.

If the results of factor analysis look useful, and you need more information than is provided in this book, you could consult Field (2000) for a more detailed guide on doing factor analysis. Tabachnick and Fidell (1996) present a much more detailed account of factor analysis, including a comparison of the relevant statistics packages.

SUMMARY

This chapter described how to get a final, reliable scale from the pool of items that your participants have responded to. This involved coding your questionnaire, making a database, and using a reliability analysis to see how strongly each item, in turn, relates to all the other items in the scale (or subscale). Those that do not relate well are removed, and the result should be a consistent, reliable scale.

Factor and principal components analysis were briefly outlined, as was item weighting.

Chapter 6

The final scale and its validation

DESCRIPTIVE STATISTICS (NORMS)

Your scale is almost complete. You have:

- a list of the items to be included;
- range, mean(s), and standard deviations (or variances, which are the square of the standard deviations)—these are the descriptive statistics proper, the norms;
- a description of the sample(s) associated with each mean;
- reliability statistics;
- established content and possibly face validity.

The preceding chapters have described how to do all of this, and so far the achievement of two types of validity (content and face) have been discussed. These are achieved at the point of developing the initial scale (see Chapter 3).

The rest of this chapter is concerned with establishing other forms of validity.

VALIDITY

Several methods of exploring validity are suggested in this section. You do not have to assess the validity of your scale on all these criteria, but it is usually advisable to achieve content (and probably face) validity, and/or at least one other type of validity.

I have suggested a particular statistical test for each type of validity, guessing the most likely scenario for the type of data involved. But if you wish to decide for yourself which test might be

Table 6.1   Selecting the right analysis to study the significance of the relationship between two variables

Dependent (outcome) variable	Independent (predictor) variable(s)	
	Categorical	Continuous
Categorical	Chi-square	Logistic regression* or Anova** or (if the categorical variable is dichotomous) t-test
Continuous	Analysis of variance (anova) or (if the categorical variable is dichotomous) t-test	Correlation

* For logistic regression, independent variables may be a mixture of continuous and categorical (dichotomous).
** But rather confusingly in this case, in anova, the categorical grouping variable is sometimes called the independent variable, and the continuous variable is sometimes called the dependent variable.

the most appropriate, consult Table 6.1, and if you are not sure what kind of data you have, consult Appendix 5.1. The presentation of statistical tests in this chapter and in Appendix 6 is simplified in the interests of clarity. If the presentation is unclear, or if you would like a better understanding of the issues involved, do consult a qualified person, or a competent book such as Clark-Carter (1997), Cramer (1993), Field (2000), Gravetter and Wallnau (1999), or Howitt and Cramer (2000).

Criterion validity

This means comparing performances on your test or scale with some criterion. For example, comparing the performances of two or more different groups of people on your test, when you could hypothesise that they should perform differently. This can be tested by carrying out an *unrelated t-test* if two groups are being compared, or a *one-way analysis of variance* (anova) if more than two groups are compared.

At this point you need to compute participants' total scores on your new scale—which you may not have done yet. Appendix 6.1 describes how to do this in SPSS.

A *t*-test would specify the grouping variable as the independent variable or group. The dependent variable would be scores on your final scale. If you had predicted the *direction* of the difference, a 1-tailed *t*-test is appropriate; if not, then the 2-tailed *t* value should be taken.

For example, in the prayer example in Figure 3.2, religious affiliation is a grouping (independent) variable, created by recoding all those who joined any religious group into one category. Religious affiliation is thus a dichotomous variable—affiliated and non-affiliated are its two values. We would expect that the religiously affiliated would have higher scores on the prayer scale than the non-affiliated, so a 1-tailed *t*-test would be appropriate. Of course, if a difference between two groups emerged in a direction *opposite* to that predicted, you would have to take the 2-tailed probability.

Appendices 6.2 and 6.4 show how to carry out a *t*-test and analysis of variance using SPSS for Windows.

When describing the results of your criterion validity testing, you would say something like:

One measure of criterion validity was tested and found to be satis-factory. Comparison was made of the total prayer scores of the non-affiliated (n=40) with the affiliated (n=60) in a convenience sample of 50 female and 50 male British undergraduate students aged 18–50 (mean age 22.5). The mean score for the affiliated sample was 22.5 (SD = 1.22), and mean for the unaffiliated sample was 13.1 (SD = 2.30), *t*(equal variances not assumed) = 21.81, df = 53.862, 1-tailed p = .000.

When describing the results of criterion validity testing, describe:

- the characteristics of those tested (age, gender, etc.);
- how they were sampled;
- the means (and standard deviations) associated with the groups;

- the value of t, degrees of freedom, whether one- or two-tailed, and probability.

If using analysis of variance rather than a t-test, as you would with more than one group, state the between-groups F ratio, degrees of freedom and probability, and the results of any testing of contrasts between groups (the section on predictive validity gives an example).

Concurrent validity—comparison with existing tests

This means looking at the performance of your participants on one or more other methods of assessing what your test is assessing.

This is potentially quite an embarrassing situation because if there is another test assessing what your scale is assessing, you have to demonstrate why your scale is necessary. This can be done by establishing that, by comparison with the standard (comparison) test, your scale is superior on one or more of the following features:

- meets reliability criteria as well or better;
- is (on other criteria of validity) as valid or has better validity;
- is as quick or quicker to administer;
- can be used on an as wide or wider range of people.
- preferable on some other attribute: For example, your test might be more interesting or less threatening than the existing standard test, and this is associated with higher completion rates.

Your test should be no worse than the standard test on any of these criteria, and it should be an improvement in at least one respect.

If there is a standard test measuring something similar to yours, and it is reliable and valid, then you can examine correlations between scores on the two tests. If there is a significant association, then your test has concurrent validity. The two tests obviously have to be completed by the same people—preferably on the same occasion (otherwise any lack of association between the two might be due to different circumstances at the time of testing).

If your participants did the standard test on a later occasion, you can add the results to your database.

You then *correlate* scores on the two tests. A method for doing this in SPSS is described in Appendix 6.3. The correlation(s) should of course be in the expected direction, and statistically significant.

In presenting the results of concurrent validity testing, you would say something like:

> One form of concurrent validity was tested and found to be satisfactory. 100 British undergraduates (50 female and 50 male, aged 19–46, mean age 22.5) completed the prayer scale, and Smith's (1932) attitudes to prayer scale [a hypothetical example]. The (Pearson) correlation was $r = 0.554$, one-tailed $p < .01$. The new prayer scale is suggested as a rapid and convenient alternative to Smith's scale, which is much longer (50 items, some of which appear archaic).

Content and face validity

This should be done when you are writing the scale, by seeing if one or more independent judges agree that your items appear to be/are about what you are trying to measure. Items that judges have reasonable doubts about, should be discarded. Obviously, if you have more than one judge, and both or all agree that an item is unclear, this strengthens the case for scrapping it.

In the case of content validity, judges should have some expertise in the *topic* of the scale, so that they are qualified to judge whether the items really *are* about what the scale is measuring. For example, in the case of measuring attitudes to prayer, judges should know something about prayer and its functions—perhaps ministers or practitioners of religion. In the case of liking for chocolate, judges should have some knowledge or experience of eating chocolate. If assessing depression, mental health professionals such as clinical psychologists, psychiatrists, or psychiatric nurses would be appropriate. Clearly, judges who know nothing about prayer, or have never tasted chocolate, or who have no dealings with depressed people, will not be appropriate.

In the case of face validity, judges should be drawn from the same population of those you propose to assess. So if you wish to assess the attitudes of soldiers with experience of battle conditions to the efficacy of prayer, or young Europeans' liking for chocolate, or levels of depression in a Canadian urban community sample, then judges should be drawn from the same populations, namely, soldiers with battle experience, young Europeans, and Canadian city dwellers. Their opinion about whether your items appear to be about the efficacy of prayer, liking for chocolate, and depression (respectively) indicates face validity.

Predictive validity

The other methods of determining validity are often more difficult to deal with.

Predictive validity is achieved if your test predicts behaviour occurring *after* testing. The main problem is the worry and time involved in following up the people who did your test, as described in Chapter 1. Nevertheless you will have to consider getting such data, if you are trying to create a test that will only be useful if it can predict performance. Sometimes follow-up data may come your way quite easily. Such data can be added to your database and analysed as follows:

- If the data consist of scores on some measure, you can correlate scores on your test with these performance scores. See Appendix 6.3 for a method of carrying out a correlation using SPSS.
- If the performance measure is binary (for example, did the people succeed or fail on something, do or not do something?), the simplest way to look at associations is to do a *t*-test using the binary performance measure as a grouping variable, and scores on your test as the dependent variable (see Appendix 6.2).
- If the performance measure is categorical, but there are more than two categories, then a one-way analysis of variance could be done, using the performance measure as a grouping variable, and scores on your measure as the dependent variable. Appendix 6.4 describes how to do this in SPSS.

To present the results of an analysis of variance, you can present an analysis of variance table if there was a fairly complex research design involving two or more grouping variables, and/or a mixed analysis of variance involving within and between-subjects effects. In a case with only one grouping variable, an anova table is not necessary; you only need to describe on one F ratio, and the results can be presented by quoting the F ratio, the two relevant figures for degrees of freedom, and the probability. For example:

> Significant differences in prayer scores went with later religious-group-joining: $F2, 97 = 431.176$, $p < .001$. Participants were 100 British undergraduates (50 female and 50 male, aged 19–46, mean age 22.5). Those who joined a campus religious group scored significantly higher than those who did not. Post-hoc comparisons (LSD) showed significant differences ($p < .05$) between those joining the two religious groups (Anglicans mean = 20.5; New Christians mean = 23.0); both these groups scored significantly higher than those not joining religious groups (mean = 13.52).

Construct validity

This is obtained when what you are measuring relates to other factors in ways that were predicted by the theory underlying the development of your test. If such a possibility arises, you should be able to carry out tests of associations between variables using correlation, unrelated t-test, analysis of variance, or methods of partialling out spurious effects described in this chapter, and in Appendix 6.

Confounded variables

Sometimes two or more variables may be confounded with each other (they co-vary) and this can affect the results of validity testing. "True" relationships can be obscured.

For example, if we found that students who believed in the efficacy of prayer were more likely to join religious groups on campus, we might begin to worry about whether this was a true effect if we noticed an age difference between those joining religious groups and those not joining. Perhaps it is really age that is related to beliefs about prayer, and not religious group membership as such? Or perhaps both factors are related to beliefs about prayer?

If you suspect that there are confounded variables in your data, select the appropriate analysis from Table 6.2. All these tests will

Table 6.2   Selecting the right analysis when there are confounded variables

Dependent (outcome) variable	Independent (predictor) variable(s)	
	Categorical	Continuous
Categorical	Loglinear analysis (Hiloglinear) or n-dimensional chi-square	Logistic regression*
Continuous	Analysis of covariance (ancova)**	Multiple regression analysis***

* For logistic regression, independent variables may be a mixture of continuous and categorical (dichotomous).
** For analysis of covariance, the covariate(s) should preferably be continuous.
*** For multiple regression analysis, independent variables may be a mixture of continuous and categorical (dichotomous).

express the "true" association between the dependent (outcome) variable and, in turn, each of the independent (predictor) variables which have been entered into the analysis, whilst taking out the "spurious" contribution of the other independent variables in the analysis.

Appendix 6.5 provides some brief further details of how to compute these, but if you wish to use any of these methods of analysis you may need to consult a textbook such as Tabachnick and Fidell (1996), a guide such as Field (2000), and/or your statistics software manual.

PRESENTING THE SCALE

Here is the checklist of points to cover when presenting your scale:

- a statement of what the scale measures
- justification for the scale (uses, advantages over existing measures)
- how the preliminary pool of items was drawn up—details of sources, sampling of sources, any special steps with respect to content or face validity
- a description of the sample used for testing
- reliability statistics

- validity statistics
- the scale itself (instructions, items or examples of items)
- descriptive statistics (norms): means, standard deviations, ranges (for different samples of participants, different sub-scales).

SUMMARY

This chapter described the final steps in presenting the scale, describing how to carry out validity testing. These put the final touches to the basic requirements of developing a scale which measures reliably what it is supposed to measure. The test should be usable by others to obtain results that can be interpreted and compared using the normative data you have produced.

Examples of test and scale presentation

These examples have been selected to illustrate some of the range of factors that can be assessed in a psychological scale. A range of topics has been used: narcissism, individual responsibility, structure of prayer, and quality of cognitive therapy. They show the sort of information that needs to be collected and presented, so that potential users can evaluate the test's usefulness to them. The examples are summaries of much longer presentations in academic journal articles and books. I have indicated points where the information presented seems inadequate. Further useful examples can be seen on the web sites of Maltby, Lewis, and Hill (p. 164), the Buros Institute (p. 163), and of course in the academic press.

EXAMPLE 1. NARCISSISTIC PERSONALITY INVENTORY (NPI)

This example is a relatively modern measure of personality. Part of the development of this measure is described quite fully in Raskin and Terry (1988), and the following points are extracted from Raskin and Terry's description.

Statement of what the scale measures

General narcissism, and seven components: authority, exhibitionism, superiority, vanity, exploitativeness, entitlement, and self-sufficiency. Definitions of narcissism are offered from DSM-III (the American Psychiatric Association's *Diagnostic and Statistical Manual of Mental Disorders*, 1980), Freud (1914/1957, 1923/1961), and Ellis (1898).

Justification for the scale

The authors offer an extensive survey of the theoretical importance of narcissism, especially in the psychoanalytic and clinical literature. The chief justification appears to be the growing recognition of the clinical importance of narcissistic personality disorder.

How the preliminary pool of items was drawn up

The DSM-III definition describes eight inter-related behaviours. These were used as a starting-point for a pool of 220 dyadic items, which were reduced to 54 items in a series of studies using the internal consistency approach (Raskin & Hall, 1979). The authors also used Emmons' (1984) principal components analytic work on the NPI as a starting-point for an examination of the distinguishable factors assessed within the NPI.

Description of the sample used for testing

Three studies are reported, all using students from the University of California. The first used 1008 participants (479 men, 529 women, aged 17–49, mean age 20 years), the second used 57 (28 men, 29 women, aged range not stated, mean age 21 years), and the third study used 127 students (65 men and 62 women, aged 17–40, mean age 19 years). Participants in the second study were paid, and participants in the third study received academic credit for participation.

Reliability statistics

Alphas (coefficient of internal consistency) are quoted as ranging from 0.80 to 0.86 across several studies. The present paper reported a principal components analysis, which produced the seven factors listed earlier—accounting for 49% of the variance, involving pruning the scale to 40 items. Each scale involved at least three marker items with loadings of 0.50 or above.

Validity statistics

A variety of construct validity studies are referred to. The study under description describes two construct validity studies investigating the relationship of full-scale narcissism and the subscales with a variety of measures from observational data, self-report, and self-description. Reported significant correlations, according with theory underlying the NPI, range from 0.17 to 0.47.

The scale

The current NPI has 40 paired items. Participants are asked to mark the member of each pair that they most agree with. For example:

A   I have a natural talent for influencing people.
B   I am not good at influencing people.
(Authority)

A   I don't care about new fads and fashions.
B   I like to start new fads and fashions.
(Exhibitionism)

A   My body is nothing special.
B   I like to look at my body.
(Vanity)

Descriptive statistics (norms)

A table gives the inter-correlations between the component sub-scales and the full scale, for the 40-item NPI. Means, standard deviations, and other statistics are reported for the full scale and the seven subscales. The mean of the full scale for the sample of 1018 students was 15.55 (SD = 6.66).

EXAMPLE 2. INDIVIDUAL RESPONSIBILITY (IR) MEASURE

This is a measure of preference for personal responsibility and Franken (1988) describes initial development of the scale.

Statement of what the scale measures

The scale measures individual responsibility: the degree to which the person prefers environments that offer personal initiative, personal freedom, and/or personal control.

Justification for the scale

The scale is introduced by suggesting the importance to occupational psychology for identifying preferences and traits that may go along with successful managerial style, as described by Peters and Waterman (1982). IR is suggested as part of a group of preferences and traits, which also includes an active-decisive style (AD) and sensation-seeking. IR is assessed together with AD (but in the description provided in this example, only IR is described).

How the preliminary pool of items was drawn up

Paired items were generated to assess whether or not the person prefers to make their own decisions versus having the decisions made by somebody else. These were alternated with items assessing decision-making style (AD).

Description of the sample used for testing

A preliminary pool of items was first tested on a sample of "about 250 students". Numbers of men and of women, and age, were unspecified. These details should have been given. This stage of testing was used to select IR and AD items that best differentiated participants with high AD from those with high IR. The IR measure was then administered to samples of 417 students (176 males, 241 females, mean age 22.6) and 349 non-students (218 males, 131 females, from 12 different occupational groups—all professional and white-collar—with mean ages from 26.6 to 36.9.

Reliability and validity statistics

Alpha (internal consistency) for the IR scale was 0.48. Note that this is low, considerably lower than 0.6, which is the lowest figure normally considered marginally acceptable. IR correlated significantly with AD ($r = 0.20$, $p < .01$) and with sensation-seeking ($r = 0.24$, $p < .01$), but not with Rotter's Internal/External Locus of Control Scale, producing mixed evidence on construct validity. Factor analytic work produced factors that corresponded "reasonably well" with the qualities the scale was designed to measure. The author regards the reliability of the IR scale and its associations with AD and sensation-seeking as modest. Means for different occupational groups suggest some degree of criterion validity: The lowest means are for retail sales and military personnel, and the highest for stockbrokers and lawyers. However, the numbers in some groups were very small—for example, only seven stockbrokers, and twelve sales assistants—which casts doubt on the representativeness of some of the samples used.

The scale

Participants are asked to select which item from each pair most describes the way they think or feel. For example:

> A   I prefer to make all my own travel arrangements.
> B   I prefer "packaged tours".
>
> A   It is the responsibility of the worker to determine how to do the job efficiently.
> B   It is the job of the manager or supervisor to determine how to do a job efficiently.

Descriptive statistics (norms)

Means for the 13 different occupational groups tested ranged from 12.33 to 15.69. Other descriptive statistics include inter-correlations of the IR with the other measures mentioned, within each occupational group.

Comment

The reliabilities and validities for this scale are not always satisfactory, but sufficient statistics are presented for this to be apparent. Beware of scales that do not present enough statistics.

EXAMPLE 3: STRUCTURE OF PRAYER SCALE

This description is based on David (1999), who drew his material from unpublished sources and conference presentations, particularly Luckow et al. (1997).

Statement of what the scale measures

The scale measures prayer behaviour. More specifically, six conceptually distinct categories of prayer are assessed: confession, petition, ritual, meditation-improvement, habit, and compassionate petition.

Justification for the scale

There has been limited interest in prayer among social scientists and psychologists, and there are no modern published measures (Brown, 1994) apart from questions in general social surveys. This measure is rapid (5–10 minutes) and assesses several categories of prayer.

How the preliminary pool of items was drawn up

Originally, items were generated with the intention of covering the full range of prayer types and habits. It is not stated by whom these items were drawn up, nor whether there were more items in the original pool than were included in the final scale(s).

Description of the sample used for testing

Items were given to a total of 986 adults in the USA, mostly students, and mostly Christian. No descriptive statistics for the samples were given, other than the numbers of participants from six different sources, five universities and Christian colleges, and a group of 166 cancer patients. Thus gender, age, and other demographic features are not known.

Reliability and validity statistics

Principal components analysis identified the six subscales listed earlier. Items with loadings of 0.3 and above were retained in each subscale. Cronbach's alpha was calculated for each subscale within each of the six samples. Of the 36 coefficients reported, 27 (75%) are above 0.70, and 34 are above 0.60. Validity issues seem generally unexplored. It is claimed that most items have face validity. It is also claimed that other (unpublished) studies have used many of the same items and have yielded a similar factor structure, but whether this constitutes evidence for validity is doubtful.

The scale

The scale has 29 items, with responses on a 6-point Likert-type scale, ranging from 1 = strongly disagree, to 6 = strongly agree. Examples:

> Petition (3 items): I must admit that I usually pray to get something.
> Habit (4 items): I usually say a prayer before each meal.
> Meditation-improvement (5 items): Prayer is a way for me to connect with my inner spirit.

Descriptive statistics (norms)

Sadly, descriptive statistics (norms) for the prayer scales are not available.

Comments

The factorial structure and internal consistency of these subscales are sufficient to warrant their use in investigations of validity. Validity and descriptive statistical information are inadequate and need to be obtained before the scale could be adopted as a useful psychometric instrument.

EXAMPLE 4. QUALITY OF COGNITIVE THERAPY SCALE (CTS)

Dobson, Shaw, and Vallis (1985) describe some of the psychometric properties of this scale.

Statement of what the scale measures

The scale involves 11 items, assessing aspects of cognitive therapy sessions on:

- agenda
- feedback
- understanding
- interpersonal effectiveness
- collaboration
- pacing and efficient use of time
- empiricism
- focus on key cognitions or behaviours
- strategy for change
- application of cognitive-behavioural techniques
- homework.

Justification for the scale

Dobson et al. stress the potential applicability of a reliable measure assessing the quality of therapy (process), and in order to evaluate outcomes.

How the preliminary pool of items was drawn up

The items appear to have been derived from the requirements of cognitive therapy specified by Beck, Rush, Shaw, and Emery (1979) and Emery, Hollon, and Bedrosian (1981), and for psychotherapy in general (Arnkoff, 1983; Beck et al., 1979; Rogers, 1957; Truax & Carkhuff, 1967).

Description of the sample used for testing

Twenty-one psychotherapists (10 psychiatrists and 11 psychologists; 14 males and 7 females) each supplied a 1-hour videotape sample of their work: 12 were tapes of ongoing therapy sessions, and 9 were initial consultations.

Four raters, all experienced and expert cognitive-behavioural therapists, rated 10 or 11 recorded therapy sessions each, such that each session was rated ("blind") by two raters. A total of 42 sets of ratings were made.

Reliability statistics

A full range of internal consistency statistics are presented. In spite of the variety of items (and the fact that the scale was proposed to measure two possibly independent dimensions), overall scale alpha = 0.95, suggesting uni-dimensionality. Only the homework items failed to produce a satisfactory item-total correlation.

Validity statistics

Apart from the apparent face and content validity of the items, this presentation does not offer evidence for validity. However, Dobson et al. do present an analysis of variance which shows that between-rater effects were not significant, while between-subject (sessions rated) effects were. This may be regarded (rather loosely) as a form of criterion validity, since it suggests that sessions differed from each other in quality—and quality could be reliably rated.

The scale

The scale involves Likert-type ratings on the 11 dimensions described previously.

Descriptive statistics (norms)

A notable drawback of the presentation is that no means (norms) are provided for the CTS.

Appendix to Chapter 2

Selecting tests

APPENDIX 2.1. GUIDELINES FOR PSYCHOLOGICAL TESTING

This appendix describes guidelines from the American Psychological Association, the British Psychological Society, and the Institute of Personnel and Development.

Standards for Educational and Psychological Tests

These standards are published jointly by the American Psychological Association, American Educational Research Association, and the National Council on Measurement in Education (1985). They appear in book form, and also in the Buros Institute's Mental Measurements Yearbook (Buros Institute, 1992). Other, briefer standards appear on the Buros Institute web site, under the ERIC/AE test locator (p. 163).

The standards are lengthy, essential for those working professionally with psychological assessment in the USA, and strongly recommended for those working professionally with psychological assessment in other countries. This brief outline is introductory; the reader is also advised to consult the standards described elsewhere in Appendix 2, and in Appendix 4.

The principal sections of the standards are:

- Standards for Tests, Manuals and Reports
- Standards for Reports of Research on Reliability and Validity
- Standards for the Use of Tests.

About 300 standards are described, each graded as

- Essential, or
- Very Desirable, or
- Desirable.

Selected essential standards are summarised below:

Standards for Tests, Manuals and Reports

A1.   A published test should be accompanied by an updated manual or other available information, in which every reasonable effort has been made to follow the recommendations of these standards.

B1.   The test, the manual, and all associated material should help users make correct interpretations of the test material, and warn against common misuses.

B2, B3, B4, B5.   The manual should state the recommended purposes and applications of the test, the characteristic(s) measured, the qualifications required for test administration and interpretation, and evidence of reliability and validity and other related research.

C1.   Directions for administration and scoring should enable duplication of the conditions under which norms, reliability, and validity were obtained.

D1.   Most tests are interpreted by comparing scores with scores made by other individuals. These are *norm-referenced* tests. Any such tests require the publication of norms in the manual.

D2.   Norms should refer to clearly defined populations.

Standards for Reports of Research on Reliability and Validity

E1.   A manual or report should present the evidence of validity for each type of inference for which test use is recommended (and any omissions in this respect should be made clear).

Detailed recommendations are given for each type of validity.

F1.   A manual or report should present evidence of reliability, including estimates of the standard error of measurement, so as to enable users to judge whether scores are sufficiently dependable for intended uses of the test (and any omissions in this respect should be made clear).

Detailed recommendations for each type of reliability.

Standards for the Use of Tests

G1. Any test user should have a knowledge of the principles of (psychological) measurement, and of the limitations of test interpretation.

H1. Choice of tests or other assessments should be based on clearly formulated goals and hypotheses.

I1, I3. The standardised procedures described in the test manual for administration and accurate scoring.

J1. A test score should be interpreted as an estimate of performance under specific circumstances, not as an absolute characteristic that will apply in other circumstances.

J5. In norm-referenced interpretations, scores must be interpreted with reference to appropriate norms.

Among *many other detailed recommendations*, users are warned against bias, and the use of obsolete material.

The British Psychological Society's Steering Committee on Test Standards

Psychological Testing: A User's Guide (1995) is obtainable from the British Psychological Society (see p. 164). This booklet has been developed by the British Psychological Society's Steering Committee on Test Standards (SCTS). The booklet:

- outlines the categories of tests (attainment, ability, disposition, etc.), and
- the settings in which psychological tests are most frequently used (educational, occupational, clinical), and
- the reasons for using psychological tests (they provide information useful for assessment and diagnosis, more efficiently than many other methods).

The booklet aims to help readers to know what to look for in a test, including:

- a statement of what the test measures
- the rationale and background
- evidence of reliability; forms of reliability are briefly described
- evidence of validity; forms of validity are briefly described
- information enabling the test scores to be evaluated
- information on whether the test has been evaluated for bias, and with what results.

The booklet goes on to discuss competence to administer and use psychological tests, and gives information on the British Psychological Society's Certificates of Competence. The booklet provides information on the responsible use of tests, including the following guidelines:

- The purpose of testing is clearly stated and communicated to all parties involved in the testing process. This includes stating the purpose and expected outcomes of testing, and reasons for using the test(s).
- The procedures for testing are clearly stated and communicated to all parties involved in the testing process. This should include a declaration of who will administer the test, and their competence, and a declaration of where the test will be administered, and the suitability of this environment.
- How the test information will be used is clearly stated and communicated to all parties involved in the testing process. This includes informing those concerned who will score the test, who will have access to the scores, how the scores will be used, and how confidentiality will be protected.
- Procedures for dealing with inquiries and complaints about the process of testing are clearly stated and communicated to all parties involved in the testing process. This includes saying who will handle enquiries and complaints, for ensuring they are competent, for ensuring that complaints will be handled fairly and ethically.

The Institute of Personnel and Development

The *IPD Guide on Psychological Testing* (1997) is obtainable from the Institute of Personnel and Development, IPD House, Camp

Road, Wimbledon, London SW19 4UX, tel.: 020 8 971 9000. This booklet covers similar ground to the British Psychological Society's *Guide to Psychological Testing*, described previously. However, the booklet is geared specifically towards the use of tests in occupational settings, in:

- recruitment and selection
- training and development
- counselling

Therefore, in addition to stressing the importance of reliability and validity, the booklet deals with factors important in the occupational setting, such as:

- Is it appropriate to use tests at all—will they provide additional, relevant information?
- When used for selection, are the tests relevant to the job and person specification, and chosen on the basis of a job analysis?
- Are those who will administer, evaluate, interpret, and feed back the results competent to do so?
- Do the tests infringe equality of opportunity (this may happen if different groups of people score differently on the test)?
- How will the results be stored and used? Test results should be evaluated carefully, in the context of other information about the person.
- Have the test norms been updated and verified within the last 5 years?

The booklet deals with important legal aspects of test use:

- Copyright laws prohibit reproduction of test materials (including transferring them into computer versions) without the supplier's permission?
- Similarly, tests may not be adapted or edited without permission. Such adaptation produces flawed test results.
- Test use should not infringe the following legislation:
  - Data Protection Act 1984
  - Sex Discrimination Act 1975
  - Sex Discrimination (NI) Order 1976 as amended
  - Race Relations Act 1976
  - Fair Employment Act (NI) 1989 as amended.

These Acts are published by HMSO (Her Majesty's Stationery Office) and may be ordered from HMSO, POB 276, London SW8 5DR, 020 7 873 9090. Implications of these Acts for employers are contained in the following:

IPM Code on Employee Data
IPM Equal Opportunities Code
IPM Recruitment Code

which may be ordered from the Institute of Personnel Management.

Other useful information on tests and testing

The CTI Psychology web site is a further useful source of information (p. 163). Select *Teaching and Learning Resources*, and then *Assessment and Testing (Psychometrics)*.

APPENDIX 2.2. PUBLISHERS OF PSYCHOLOGICAL TESTS

A brief list is given below. More comprehensive lists appear in the following sources:

- Gregory, R. (1996). Appendix B of: *Psychological Testing: History, Principles, Applications*. Boston: Allyn & Bacon.
- British Psychological Society Steering Committee on Test Standards (1999). *Non-evaluative UK Test Publishers' List*. Leicester, UK: British Psychological Society.
- Buros Institute of Mental Measurement, *The Mental Measurement Yearbooks*. Highland Park, NJ: Gryphon Press. (These have been published annually for many years. Much of the information can now be obtained electronically—see next.)
- Buros Institute of Mental Measurement web site, Buros/ERIC Test Publisher Directory—see p. 163.

Brief list of test publishers

Consulting Psychologists Press Inc., PO Box 10096, Palo Alto, California 94303, USA.

Educational and Industrial Testing Service (EDITS), PO Box 7234, San Diego, California 92107, USA.

Hodder Headline, PO Box 702, Dunton Green, Sevenoaks, Kent TN13 2YD, UK (tel.: 01732 450111).

Jossey-Bass, 615 Montgomery Street, San Francisco, CA 94111, USA.

NFER (National Foundation for Educational Research), NFER Nelson Publishing Company Ltd, Darville House, 2 Oxford Road East, Windsor, Berks SL4 1DF, UK (tel.: 01753 858961; fax: 01753 856830).

Oxford Psychologists Press Ltd, Lambourne House, 311–321 Banbury Road, Oxford OX2 7JH, UK (tel.: 01865 510203; fax: 01865 310368).

Psychological Corporation, 555 Academic Court, San Antonio, TX 78204-2498, USA.

Psychological Corporation Ltd, 24–28 Oval Road, London NW1 7DX (tel.: 020 7 424 4456).

Saville & Holdsworth Ltd, 3 AC Court, High Street, Thames Ditton, Surrey KT7 0SR, UK (tel.: 020 8 398 4170).

APPENDIX 2.3. MEASURES INCLUDED IN THE NATIONAL FOUNDATION FOR EDUCATIONAL RESEARCH (NFER) PORTFOLIOS

These portfolios are obtainable from NFER (address in Appendix 2.2). Tests in the portfolio may be photocopied for use by members of the purchasing institution, and the portfolio is an economical alternative to purchase of commercially published tests, for those working in institutions which have purchased the portfolios.

Mental Health Portfolio

General distress:
• The General Heath Questionnaire

Anxiety:
- The Fear Questionnaire
- The Mobility Inventory for Agoraphobia
- The Clinical Anxiety Scale
- The Padua Inventory

Stress, coping, and social support:
- Hassles and Uplifts Scales
- The Significant Others Scale
- The Coping Responses Inventory

Habit disorder:
- The Morgan-Russell Assessment Schedule
- The Body Shape Questionnaire
- The Short Alcohol Dependence Scale

Psychological adjustment to illness:
- McGill Pain Questionnaire

Interpersonal difficulties:
- Social Activities and Distress Scale
- Inventory of Interpersonal Problems
- The Golombok Rust Inventory of Sexual Satisfaction
- The Golombok Rust Inventory of Marital State

Health Psychology Portfolio

Pain and pain behaviours:
- McGill Pain Questionnaire (MPQ)
- Pain Intensity Rating Scales:
    i   Verbal rating scales
    ii   Box scales
    iii Numerical rating scales
    iv   Visual analogue scales
- UAB Pain Behaviour Scale
- Beliefs about Pain Control Questionnaire (BPCQ)
- Pain Coping Strategies Questionnaire (CSQ)
- Varni-Thompson Paediatric Pain Questionnaire (PPQ)

Stress, emotions, and life events:
- The Hospital Anxiety and Depression Scale (HADS)

- General Health Questionnaire (GHQ-12)
- Centre for Epidemiological Studies Depression Scale (CES-D)
- Perceived Stress Scale (PSS)

Coping:
- COPE
- Mental Adjustment to Cancer Scale

Social support:
- Short Form of Social Support Questionnaire (SSQ-6)
- Significant Others Scale (SOS)

Health status and health-related quality of life:
- Perceived Health Status: Single-item measures
  - a Visual Analogue Scale (VAS)
  - b Verbal Rating Scales of Health Status (VRS)
- Satisfaction with Life Scale (SWLS)
- Acceptance of Illness Scale (AIS)
- Quality of Adjusted Life Year Index (QALY)
- Illness-specific measures
  - a Arthritis Impact Measurement Scale (AIMS)
  - b Rotterdam Symptom Check List (RSCL)

Illness, symptoms, disability, recovery:
- Barthel Index
- Functional Limitations Profile (FLP)
- Measuring Symptoms

Expectation, experience, and evaluation of health care:
- Attitudes Towards Doctors and Medicine Scale
- Patient Request Form
- Krantz Health Opinion Survey (HOS)
- Cancer Attitude Inventory (CAS)
- Prejudicial Evaluation and Social Interaction Scale (PESIS)
- Medical Interview Satisfaction Scale (MISS)

Individual and demographic differences:
- Framingham Type A Behaviour Pattern Measure
- Framingham Anger Measure
- Courtauld Emotional Control Scale (CECS)
- Marlowe-Crowne Scale

- Positive and Negative Affect Schedule (PANAS)
- Pennebaker Inventory of Limbic Languidness (PILL)
- Rosenberg Self-Esteem Scale (RSES)
- Life Orientation Test (LOT)

Causal and control beliefs:
- Multidimensional Health Locus of Control Scale (MHLC)
- Children's Health Locus of Control Scale (Child HLC)
- Perceived Control of Insulin Dependent Diabetes
- Recovery Locus of Control Scale (RLOC)
- Self-efficacy measurement:
  a   Specific Self-efficacy Beliefs
  b   Generalised Self-efficacy Scale
- Approaches to the measurement of health-related attributions:
  a   Forced choice ratings
  b   Spontaneous
  c   Attributional style

Beliefs and knowledge about health and illness:
- Health Value Scale
- Model-based approaches to measurement, based on:
  a   The Health Belief Model
  b   Theory of Reasoned Action
  c   Illness Representation Model
- Health Knowledge

Health-related behaviour:
- General Preventive Behaviours Checklist (GPBH)
- Reported Health Behaviours Checklist
- Self-monitoring techniques

Child Psychology Portfolio

Health and illness in childhood
- Children's Headache Assessment Scale
- Functional Disability Inventory (FDI)
- Child Health-Related Quality of Life (CQOL)
- Varni-Thompson Paediatric Pain Questionnaire (PPQ)
- Children's Health Locus of Control (CHLC)
- Revised Measure of Behavioural Upset in Medical Patients (BUMP-R)

Social behaviour and competence in childhood:
- Taxonomy of Problem Situations (TOPS)
- Prosocial Behaviour Questionnaire (PBQ)
- Kidscope
- Locus of Control Scale for Children
- Life in School Checklist
- Target Child Observation (TCO)

Emotional and behavioural problems in children:
- Revised Rutter Parent Scale for Preschool Children
- Revised Rutter Teacher/Nursery Staff Scale for Preschool Children
- Revised Rutter Parent Scale for School-Age Children
- Revised Rutter Teacher Scale for School-Age Children
- Behavioural Screening Questionnaire (BSQ)
- The Behaviour Checklist (BCL)
- Werry-Weiss-Peters Activity Rating Scale

Anxiety, depression and post-traumatic stress in childhood:
- The Spence Children's Anxiety Scale (SCAS)
- The Fear Survey Schedule for Children—Revised (FSSC-R)
- The Children's Impact of Events Scale (IES)
- The Birleson Depression Scale

Families and relationships:
- Darlington Family Assessment System (DAFS)
- The Family Grid
- The Family Health Scales (FHS)
- The Beavers Interactional Scales and Family Competence Scale

Parental coping and support:
- Family Crisis Oriented Personal Evaluation Scales (F-COPES)
- Coping Health Inventory for Parents (CHIP)
- Family Support Scale (FSS)
- Social Support Resources Scale (SSR)
- Questionnaire on Resources and Stress—Friedrich Short-Form (QRS-F)

APPENDIX 2.4. THE BRITISH PSYCHOLOGICAL SOCIETY'S CERTIFICATES OF COMPETENCE IN OCCUPATIONAL TESTING

These certificates are designed for both non-psychologists who need to use psychological tests in their professional work. The British Psychological Society's Steering Committee on Test Standards now considers them necessary even for those who already hold, or who expect to gain a psychology degree, since their training in psychometrics may be inadequate.

Further details of these certificates may be obtained from: The Register of Competence in Occupational Testing, The British Psychological Society, St Andrews House, 49 Princess Road East, Leicester LE1 7DR (tel.: 0116 252 9530; email: rcot@bps.org.uk). The British Psychological Society issues a number of free leaflets and booklets:

- *A General Information Pack about the Level A Certificate in Occupational Testing*
- *Psychological Testing: A User's Guide*
- *Questions and Answers about Psychological Testing*
- *Non-evaluative List of UK Test Publishers*
- Leaflet describing the *BPS Review of Ability and Aptitude Tests (Level A) for use in Occupational Settings*
- Leaflet describing the *BPS Review of Personality Assessment Instruments (Level B) for use in Occupational Settings.*

Further details of relevant tests, courses, and services are maintained in a (rather expensive) publication called the *Selection and Development Review*, issued every two months by the BPS Division of Occupational Psychology. The direct line to the Register of Competence in Occupational Testing (tel.: 0116 252 9530) may be able to offer some information about where to get training. This training may be offered by a local university psychology department. Note that the skills taught do *not* involve test or scale *construction*; the certificates cover the knowledge and skills required to understand, evaluate, administer, score, interpret, and feed back psychological tests and test results.

Level A

This level covers the general foundations of testing, and the performance skills associated with test administration and interpretation for group *ability tests*. The level A units cover:

- defining assessment needs;
- basic principles of scaling and standardisation;
- importance of reliability and validity;
- deciding when psychological tests should or should not be used as part of an assessment process;
- administering tests to one or more candidates and dealing with scoring procedures;
- making appropriate use of test results and providing accurate written and oral feedback to clients and candidates;
- maintaining security and confidentiality of the test materials and the test data.

Level B

This level (there are two level B qualifications) builds on level A competencies, covering personality assessment, and the interpretation and use of *personality tests*. An Intermediate level B certificate is gained by obtaining a level A certificate, and then a Foundation course covering theory, personality assessment, administration, interpretation, and feedback. This is followed by further units (for a full Level B certificate) in specific test use and interpretation, and in test choice, covering issues such as validity, reliability, and computer-based assessment.

APPENDIX 2.5. SOME USEFUL TESTS: AN INTRODUCTORY REVIEW

The following short survey introduces a small selection of widely used tests and scales, and mentions some of their advantages and shortcomings. This survey could be useful if you are unfamiliar with the variety of tests and scales available, and have no familiarity with the more commonly used measures. It does not claim to be comprehensive, or even to give a systematic description of the tests covered. The survey is designed to draw your attention to some commonly used tests, and some of their features. Chapter 2 offers advice on how to conduct a comprehensive search.

Note the following:

- Make clear to yourself *what you want to assess* (best to write it down). Think and decide whether the test(s) you are interested in really do assess what you want to assess.
- Most of the tests and scales discussed have *user restrictions* (see Chapter 2). If you are a student working under qualified supervision, you may be able to use many of them nevertheless, provided no special training is required. Note that it may take some effort to discover whether there are user restrictions. A test published in an academic journal may not necessarily be "public domain", since subsequently the author may have published commercially. Check any stock of published tests you may have access to, check test publishers' catalogues, and if the test does not appear to be published, write to the author for permission to reproduce and to use it. The author's address for correspondence is given in the journal, and email addresses are now commonly given.
- *Who are you testing?* The tests and measures discussed later are suitable for use with literate English-speaking adults. If you are working with children, those with disabling conditions, cultural minorities, or any other special groups, you will need to consult with those who have experience in doing assessments of the group(s) concerned.
- If a test sounds likely, check the test handbook or other published description for *more details*. Do the types of reliability and validity reported meet your needs? For example if you were looking for a measure that was sensitive to changes as a result of external events, you would probably be more interested in internal consistency and would probably avoid a test with high test–retest reliability (suggesting that it may not readily reflect change).

I have divided the measures into four groups:

1   Personality, mood, and psychopathology.
2   Social attitudes and cognitions.

3 Other individual differences.
4 Social desirability.

For fuller information on each test, consult the sources in Appendix section 2.2 (who will give supplier details), or the handbook or published journal article describing the test. The tests described have (unless otherwise stated) met at least minimal requirements for reliability and validity as follows:

Reliability: a reported coefficient of at least 0.70 for the scale and for each of any subscales, or adequate factor-analytic derivation;

Validity: adequate and appropriate evidence of at least one of the following forms of validity: Concurrent, criterion, predictive, construct, in addition to face and construct validity where these are appropriate.

Measures of personality, mood, and psychopathology

The Multiple Affect Adjective Check List (MAACL; Zuckerman & Lubin, 1963)

The state version (there is also a trait version) covers three common distress states: depression, anxiety, and hostility. It looks formidable, with well over 100 items, but all participants have to do is tick the words that apply to them, so it can be completed quite rapidly. However, you may have to reassure people that it *does* only take a few moments. It does have some positive mood words on it, which makes it less threatening, but positive mood is not actually assessed—failures to check positive mood words contribute to the negative mood (distress) score. This test has been validated against clinical groups but is not in itself a measure of clinical state. Some words (such as "gay") are ambiguous or culturally loaded. The advantages of the measure are that it does assess hostility as well as the more commonly examined depression and anxiety, it is quick to do (in spite of appearances), and it has been very well-researched.

The Beck Depression Inventory (BDI; Beck & Steer, 1987)

Of all negative states, depression is probably the most heavily researched, and of all measures of depression, this is probably the most popular. The measure has been well-researched, and it does give some idea of *clinical* status. The two main complaints I have heard are that some of the questions are rather intrusive (and therefore the measure may be seen as threatening), and it is rather an expensive test. The advantages are relative speed of administration (compared to a "proper" clinical interview and assessment), and lots of published research for you to compare your data with. In view of the expense and the ethical problems, I would avoid this scale unless you really need a measure of clinical state, and you prefer it to the HAD (described next).

The Hospital Anxiety and Depression Scale (HAD; Zigmond & Snaith, 1983)

This has been less widely used than the BDI or the MAACL. It is cheaper than either (you can get it on the Mental Health Portfolio: see Appendix 2.3). It also quick, less threatening than the BDI, and the authors have tried to select items to assess depression that are least heavily contaminated by anxiety (and vice versa), and that are unlikely to be contaminated by the presence of physical illness. This is a useful feature since the co-occurrence of depression and anxiety with each other and with physical illness has been a problem for research and assessment of both these very unpleasant conditions. The term "hospital" in the title is a bit misleading; the measure is perfectly appropriate for community and other samples. Although this has not been as popular as the previous two measures, it is becoming more widely used, and there is plenty of published material available for comparison. Validity is reported to be good; the only reliability analysis is of internal consistency, with item-subscale-total correlations ranging from 0.3 to 0.76 (some coefficients are rather low).

The Eysenck Personality Questionnaire (EPQ; Eysenck & Eysenck, 1975)

This test is developed from earlier tests in a series by the Eysenck team in London (Eysenck & Eysenck, 1964). The main traits assessed are Neuroticism (N) and Extraversion-Introversion (E), but scores on a Lie scale (L) (a social desirability measure) and a P (Psychoticism and/or Psychopathy) score may also be obtained. The measures are quick to administer, and do not need special training, and although not free, either test is relatively inexpensive compared to some commercially available tests of personality. I have never heard grumbles about these tests being threatening or intrusive, though I have some disquiet about some of the P-scale items. The tests have good psychometric properties—as indeed they should, since the items were originally selected for their properties in discriminating between clinical and non-clinical groups, and the traits measured were derived by factor analysis. Statistically these tests are sound, and they have some user-friendly features for both testers and for those being tested. They have been widely researched. However, there are some disadvantages. The P measure is not very useful, and it is not very clear what is being measured: Both psychoticism and psychopathy seem to be involved. The N measure is mixture of items that appear to gauge depression and anxiety, so one is not getting a pure measure of either. My most serious concern is that the work necessary to establish whether N is truly a measure of trait rather than state has not been done. High scores on N may reflect transient states. Research using the EPI and related scales, however, has been interpreted as if this was not a possibility. The L scale deserves to be published in its own right. It is a short, and user-friendly social desirability measure, much easier to use than any of the social desirability measures that have been published as such.

Extraversion and neuroticism are popular candidates for inclusion in the "Big Five" major personality factors, of which the other most commonly included traits are agreeableness, conscientiousness, and openness (Goldberg, 1990; McCrae & Costa, 1985).

The Minnesota Multiphasic Personality Inventory (MMPI; Hathaway & McKinley, 1943, 1967)

This is possibly the most massively popular of personality tests: I found it referred to about 1500 times in PsychLit. Psychometric properties are good. The test can be group-administered, and is reasonably straightforward to score, though the test is quite a long one. There are 13 scales, assessing (among other things) Depression,

Masculinity-Femininity, Schizophrenia, and Social desirability (Lie scale).

The Myers-Briggs Type Indicator (MBTI; Myers & McCaulley, 1985)

The distributors suggest that special training is required to administer and score this test. It has good psychometric properties and is very popular particular among occupational psychologists, for use in advising people in which types of occupation they may find themselves most comfortable, for example. The test is based on Jung's (1923) theory of personality types, and assesses introversion-extraversion (I and E), sensing-intuition (S and N), thinking-feeling (T and F), and impulse-judgement (P and J). The fact that special (and quite expensive) training is supposed to be needed to administer this test is a bit ridiculous, but the test and its results are very attractive and well-liked. Test manuals include delightful profiles of work and relationships styles which are expressed positively, i.e., non-judgementally and non-pejoratively.

16PF (Sixteen Personality Factors Questionnaire) (Cattell, 1965; Cattell, Eber, & Tatsuoka, 1970)

The test is based on Cattell's important factor-analytic work on personality, and it is quite quick and straightforward to administer and to complete. The final result is an interesting personality profile, which can be shown to the testee. One snag is that some of the 16 personality factors assessed have rather unintelligible names such as "premsia", "alaxia" and "praxermia". Unless you use the test a great deal, you may have trouble remembering what they mean and explaining them to testees: More popular terms are on offer, but some of them are a bit uncomplimentary—most people would not be pleased to learn that the test they just kindly did for you revealed them to be "less intelligent", "suspicious", of "low ego-strength", or even "group-tied". It is of interest that one of the factors assessed is intelligence, and this test may be the answer if you want a quick measure of intelligence, in conjunction with some information about personality.

Self-esteem

Coopersmith's (1967) scale was developed for use with children, and adults would find it a bit childish. The best choice for use with adults is probably *Rosenberg*'s (1965) scale, but it is not a perfect choice. Adults that I have tested have found it rather threatening and intrusive. It was originally developed as a Guttman-type scale (constructed using methods other than those described in this book, and meeting different reliability criteria). Scoring is described in Burns' (1979) excellent review of self-concept measures as "confusing". However, many researchers seem to use it as a Likert-type scale, and Rosenberg (1989) reported that this was superior. It is a widely used measure, though the Health Psychology Portfolio description reports that there are few available psychometric data. There are longer self-concept measures, for example the *Tennessee Self-Concept Scale* (Fitts, 1964), which assesses different aspects of self-esteem (moral, physical, social, etc.). The latter test is rather time-consuming to complete and to score, and expensive to buy.

Projective tests

There are a number of projective tests and techniques available. The basic idea of all of them is to present the testee with some "stimulus"—usually a picture, or the beginning of a story—and ask them to describe or complete it. The participants' "responses" are scored for the presence of themes of interest to the tester, and the theory is that people project their wishes or preoccupations into the material that they produce. The most famous of these tests is the *Rorschach* ("Ink-blot") personality test, in which people are shown a series of patterns made by blotting coloured inks onto paper, and asked to describe them. The Rorschach and other projective tests have a reputation for poor reliability. They generally need special training, in order to achieve scoring that is as reliable as possible. In spite of the massive popularity of the Rorschach, this and other projective tests are probably generally best left to their devotees.

Type A behaviour

This is assessed by a self-report measure, the *Jenkins Activity Survey* (Jenkins, Zyzanski, & Rosenman, 1978, 1979). It assesses the so-called "coronary-prone personality" (competitive, impatient, sense of urgency, drive for success). Although there are scientific disputes surrounding the findings of the team which developed this scale, the measure continues to be popular and is not difficult to use or to score. Conventional reliability statistics (alpha) are suggested to be inappropriate because the variety of behaviours and beliefs included in the measure. The item reliabilities presented range from 0.39 to 0.79 (test–retest), and 0.27–0.75 (squared multiple correlation coefficient), so in fact some of the reliability statistics are satisfactory. The most interesting validity evidence is that high scorers were nearly twice as likely to develop coronary heart disease over a 4-year period than were low scorers. An alternative suggestion about the coronary-prone personality is that it is the impatient, angry features of "Type A" that are crucial. The *Framingham Anger Measure* was designed to tap these features (Haynes, 1978).

Measures of social attitudes and cognitions

Authoritarianism: California F (Adorno, Frenkel-Brunswick, Levinson, & Sanford, 1950)

This is the justly famous traditional measure of authoritarianism. The "F" stands for "Potentiality for Fascism". It is one of several scales developed in the late 1940s by a team of social scientists in the USA, refugees from Nazi Germany. The F scale is as much a measure of beliefs and/or personality as it is of attitudes. It is supposed to assess such traits as concern with power in social relationships, anti-intraception and superstition, and it relates well to "purer" measures of social attitudes assessing anti-semitism, ethnocentrism (belief in the superiority of one's own cultural group), and political and economic conservatism (anti-welfare and anti-equal rights). The F scale has attracted much criticism, including concern about its applicability to the study of left-wing authoritarianism, and concern about the fact that none of the items are "negatively worded (reverse-meaning)". The scale is hardly a contemporary one, but I find it surprising that most of the items still sound relevant and intelligible.

Wilson-Patterson C (Conservatism) (Wilson & Patterson, 1968)

This is a more modern measure of conservatism in social attitudes and beliefs than the California F. Some of the items may be found puzzling or dated by you or by testees, such as fluoridation, pyjama parties, birching, and learning Latin, but I know of no more modern measure. This measure has good psychometric properties, it is delightfully easy to administer and to score, and in spite of the momentary bewilderment that may be caused by some items, I have found that people appear to enjoy completing this scale, which is quick and quite interesting. Psychometric properties are good. Even the bewildering items cause amusement and interest, rather than the anger or fear which may be provoked by some items on some scales.

Sex roles: Burns Life Styles for Women (Burns, 1974)

This measure assesses the extent to which the person feels that it is appropriate for women to pursue a career regardless of other commitments, or whether women should prioritise marriage, homemaking, and child-care. It was developed at a time when "feminism" was a hot topic of debate, and it still taps concerns that are important to many women, especially the more highly educated. The scale would not be appropriate for use in less privileged groups. The scale is not really appropriate for use on men either, although the author suggests that it can be administered to men by asking them to say how their ideal woman should think. The men tested by Burns certainly had a more "traditional" view of women's life-styles than did the women, but this may have been because of the way men were asked to complete the scale. It is quick to do, easy to administer (when testing those for whom it is appropriate, i.e., middle-class women), easy to score, quite interesting, and not apparently too threatening. Reliability is good. The *Bem Sex Role Inventory* (Bem, 1974) assesses psychological masculinity, femininity, and androgyny. People are asked to say whether they feel stereotypically masculine or feminine personality characteristics (adjectives) apply to them. The test has good psychometric properties and has been very popular.

Religion

A number of aspects of religious belief, experience, and feeling have been assessed. Many now appear in Hill and Hood's (1999) useful *Measures of Religiosity*. The most useful measures, in terms of their relations to other factors, are probably:

- *The Religious Life Inventory* (Batson, Schoenrade, & Ventis, 1993), which assesses *extrinsic, intrinsic, and quest* religious orientation. This scale is based on Batson's (1976) factor-analytic work using items developed by earlier workers.
- Spiritual support (Maton, 1989): Spiritual support is suggested to be a stress-buffering factor. The scale is delightfully brief, but nevertheless has a very high reported reliability, and the validity work is impressive.
- A *religious experience* measure: Hood's (1975) measure has several subscales, which survived factor analysis satisfactorily. Construct validity is satisfactory. The scale measures reported mystical-type experiences.
- Religious affiliation, religious practice and attendance, and other religious factors should be assessed in questionnaire measures developed to suit the groups investigated. It is normally very difficult to use religion measures on groups other than those for which they were developed: For example, Moslems, Jews, and other non-Christians get very uptight when asked about church attendance, or even "attendance" at "place of worship" (in some religions, "worship" especially by women is done mainly at home). Professing agnostics are another group that need special attention when assessing religion. You will therefore probably have to develop your own set of questions, or use a questionnaire developed by someone else who has worked on the same group.

Values

The *Allport-Vernon Study of Values* (Allport & Vernon, 1960) uses a forced-choice format and assesses people on self-reported interest in several general areas of activity (social, religious, political, etc.), while *Rokeach*'s (1969) checklist involves more specific values (such as salvation, forgiving) grouped under two general headings (Means, or instrumental, and Ends, or terminal). Both measures seem to be non-threatening, and quite thought-provoking. The forced-choice format of the Allport-Vernon does not reveal if a person has a generally high (or generally low) interest in all the areas examined. The measure just reveals *comparative* levels of self-reported interest in different areas, for example whether the person regards "Art" as more important than, say, their social life. Some participants may find it annoying to have to be forced to choose between two equally desirable or undesirable alternatives. This is a general problem with the forced-choice format whenever it is used to assess opinions, values, or other non-factual constructs.

Social support

This is an important area of current investigation. The *Quality of Relationships Inventory* (QRI; Pierce, Sarason, & Sarason, 1991) and the *Significant Others Scale* (SOS; Power, Champion, & Aris, 1988) are both usable measures, with good psychometric properties. The QRI is available on application to the authors, while the SOS is available in the Mental Health Portfolio. The QRI uses a Likert format, and assesses support (emotional), conflict, and depth in a given relationship. The SOS assesses emotional and practical support, both perceived and ideal, in a given relationship, and has the advantage of a delightfully brief form (4 items) as well as a longer form.

Locus of control

This is causal expectancy: the extent to which the person feels that events are caused by internal or external factors. *Levinson*'s (1973) and *Rotter*'s (1966) generalised scales are both still useful measures of generalised locus of control. Levinson's measure is probably more useful in that it distinguishes between two types of external locus of control: luck and chance on the one hand, and powerful others. Some investigators, however, prefer to use measures that are specific to the area of behaviour under investigation.

Need achievement

In the classical research, achievement-related motives and needs (need for achievement, fear of failure, fear of success) were assessed by projective tests, which often have reliability problems, and which require training. Attempts have been made to develop scales assessing need achievement, for example *Smith* (1973). My experience of using Smith's scale has been that it is easy to deal with, but unfortunately does not give very good discrimination between testees in groups of students (students get a moderately high score). It may give a wider range of scores in the general population. Indeed, Smith reported a significant difference in scores between volunteer testees and men listed in "Who's Who". Smith's reliability analysis shows only item-total correlations—rather low ones—and a rather unimpressive split-half reliability of 0.56. The literature on need achievement has reflected only low associations between need achievement and actual achievement in men, and no consistent associations for women at all. It is therefore unlikely that anyone would be considering assessing need achievement for assessment purposes when there is no measure with good predictive validity. For research—and assessment—purposes, your best bet might be to develop an achievement-need scale *specific* to the domain of achievement you are interested in. Smith's test could be useful in circumstances where a quick and friendly measure of general need-achievement is needed, provided the success or failure of your study does not hinge solely on this test. Another possibility is the measure of the *Protestant Work Ethic* (Furnham, 1984).

Measures of other individual differences

Intelligence

The measurement of intelligence is a controversial and specialised field. For an estimate of IQ (intelligence quotient) to be made, lengthy sessions of individual testing are normally required, using the *Wechsler Adult Intelligence Scale* (WAIS; Wechsler, 1955), the newer *British Ability Scales* (BAS; Elliott, 1983), or the older *Stanford-Binet*. The constructors of the BAS took into account important theoretical contributions to the understanding of the development of intelligence (notably Piagetian). All these tests are expensive and require special training, and they are normally only used for assessments carried out by clinical or educational psychologists. If you have not been introduced to the field, you may not be aware that assessments of cognitive functioning (unlike most assessments of personality, attitudes, and values) require quite specialist equipment. Tests involve a fascinating array of props: coloured blocks, stopwatches, mazes, jigsaw puzzles—you need to be quite strong to carry the box of goods to the testing site, and very deft and well-practised to record answers, to get out and arrange the next set of equipment for the next test, while checking the details in the test manual, and while giving feedback and encouragement to the testee, before the testee gets bored or wound up. (Personality and attitude testing, by contrast, normally requires the testee to read each item and write down their response, or, at most, the tester to read out the items and write down the responses).

Useful, more rapid, group-administered tests of intelligence are available, for example those developed by Alice *Heim* (Heim, 1968, 1970; Heim, Watts, & Simmons, 1983). These tests contain separate measures of verbal, numerical, and non-verbal–visual-spatial abilities. When administering these or other group tests, bear in mind that the testee can see how many items there are, and that some look impossible—this does not happen with individually administered tests, where the tester brings out the items one at a time. Testees need to be reassured that the test is designed to be virtually impossible to complete, otherwise they may find the whole experience depressing and frustrating. The *AH5* and *AH6* are for adults of higher ability, and the *AH4* covers the general range of adult ability. Another useful group test of intelligence is *Raven's Progressive Matrices* test (Raven, Raven, & Court, 1993). This involves abstract designs, each of which involves a rational series, and from which a part has been removed. The testee selects the correct missing part from several alternatives. The advantage of this test is that it involves no (overt) verbal responses, and is therefore more suitable than conventional tests for people with language difficulties, such as the deaf.

Stress

In popular parlance, stress is a state, but among psychologists, the term stress is generally used to describe a set of conditions which involve a change to customary modes of behaviour, and which a person *may* not have the resources to cope with. An early and popular stress measurement scale was the *Holmes-Rahe Social Readjustment Scale* (Holmes & Rahe, 1967). This lists a number of types of life-event (such as birthdays, violations of the law, trouble with-in-laws) and people are asked to indicate which have happened to them or to those close to them in the previous year (or in whatever period is appropriate). Each event has a weighting, an agreed index of the "average" severity of that event, and a person's score is the total of the weightings of those events they have experienced. The main problem with the Holmes-Rahe scale is that one has no idea of how any event actually impacted on the person in practice (trouble with in-laws could range from a disabling assault, to a mild disagreement about the colour-scheme for new carpets, which was eventually resolved), and thus how much their life was disrupted. Another problem with the Holmes-Rahe is that considerable research effort showed poor predictive validity. A better modern alternative might be the *Hassles and Uplifts Scale* (which can be administered as two separate scales) (Kanner, Coyne, Schaefer, & Lazarus, 1981; available in the Mental Health Portfolio; see Appendix 2.3). This measure has been claimed to be better at predicting distress and illness outcomes than the Holmes-Rahe, but your testees may get irritated and resentful because of its length and repetitiousness, even if you use only the Hassles part (both scales together have over 250 items). So-called *context-sensitive* stress measures (the original one is the *Life Events and Difficulties Schedule*: Brown & Harris, 1978) are probably the best predictors of distress and illness outcomes, and they are liked by interviewees. They are, however, extremely labour-intensive, typically requiring an interview of well over an hour and sometimes several hours, and require lengthy training both in interviewing and coding, and are therefore not advised for run-of-the-mill use.

Psychotherapy

There has been a development of attempts to monitor and measure the quality of therapy, and to assess outcome. Outcome measures will depend to an extent on the type of therapy, as therapeutic interventions are on different levels and many effects would be specific to some types of therapy only. Those investigating therapeutic outcome, however, will probably want to include perhaps one measure of "minor" psychiatric morbidity, distress, or personality (such as the MAACL, HAD, EPI or EPQ, 16PF). *Dobson* et al.'s measure (described in Appendix 2.1) was developed by using observer ratings, but this and similar measures could be used both by clients and therapists.

Health

Many measures have been developed in the rapidly-expanding area of health psychology, including the classic *McGill Pain*

Questionnaire (MPQ; Melzack, 1975) assessing quality and intensity of pain, measures of *health beliefs* (for example, Bradley et al., 1987; Given, Given, Gallin, & Condon, 1983), *condition-specific measures of locus of control* (for example, Bradley et al., 1987), and *Quality of Life* (see the Health Psychology Portfolio described in Appendix 2.3). There is now a wide range of health-related measures in the Health Psychology Portfolio. These measures are listed in Appendix 2.3.

Children

The psychometric testing of children is a specialised field. Generally, questionnaires suitable for adults should not be used on individuals aged 15 and under. Many adult questionnaires have only been developed and normed for use on people aged 18, or 21, and over, and should not be used with younger people. Tests suitable for use with children and young adolescents normally require parental permission before they can be administered. If used in a school setting, school permission will be needed as well. Supervised training would be needed or strongly advised. Some tests suitable for use with children and young adolescents are in the Child Psychology Portfolio and are listed in Appendix 2.3.

Measures of social desirability

This small group of tests was developed to address a very interesting concern of psychometricians. There are a number of ways in which answers to tests, scales, and other psychological measures may be affected by so-called "response biases". One response bias goes by the grand name of "acquiescence response set", and also the more intelligible name "yea-saying". It was briefly discussed in Chapter 3. There, it was advised that it was often useful to write some items that were negatively worded (reverse-meaning), to deal with any tendency that people may have to agree with anything, especially if it comes from an official-looking source. Chapter 3 also discussed social desirability, the tendency to give answers or to endorse responses that appear to be socially desirable, correct, or "good" in some other way, but which may not be the best reflection of the person's feelings or beliefs. Attempts have been made to assess social desirability, and, although they are somewhat culture-bound, there are occasions when one of the following measures (or another social desirability measure) may be useful.

Lie scales

The short L (Lie) scale is incorporated in the EPI (see earlier), and, although it is a good measure of social desirability, it may not be worthwhile unless you want to assess Neuroticism or Introversion-Extraversion (also assessed in the EPI). The *Minnesota Multiphasic Personality Inventory* (MMPI) also incorporates a *Lie scale*; the MMPI is a massive test and clearly it is even less worth administering the whole test for the sake of the Lie scale score.

Marlowe-Crowne SDS (Social Desirability Scale) (Crowne & Marlowe, 1960)

This scale was developed to avoid the problem that responses to social desirability items may be contaminated by psychopathology. The scale has good psychometric properties, and was shown to be less strongly related to several measures of psychopathology than the *Edwards SDS* (Social Desirability Scale; Edwards, 1957). Although it looks a bit long (and therefore daunting) it does not take long to do because people just have to tick those items that are generally applicable to them, and the items come over as interesting and thought-provoking ("I have never intensely disliked anyone") rather than threatening.

Ethical guidelines

There are a number of academic and professional organisations offering ethical guidelines for testing and research. The essential points of ethics appear in the text of Chapters 2, 3, and 4. This appendix offers further details of some of these professional guidelines, as follows:

- The American Psychological Association Standards for Educational and Psychological Tests. These are very lengthy, being published in book form. They also appear in the Buros Mental Measurements Yearbook. (Appendix 2.1 offers a summary of the main features.)
- The Australian Psychological Society offers concise guidelines for administering, scoring, and interpreting tests. Extracts appear in Appendices 4.1, 4.2, and 4.3.
- A concise statement of the minimal requirements for good practice in research involving human participants is quoted in Appendix 4.4 (guidance notes from the Ethical Committee of Royal Holloway University of London).
- The Medical Research Council (Great Britain) offers a useful booklet of guidelines for research using medical procedures or patients, mentioned in Appendix 4.5.

APPENDIX 4.1. THE AUSTRALIAN PSYCHOLOGICAL SOCIETY'S GUIDELINES FOR THE USE OF PSYCHOLOGICAL TESTS

The *Guidelines for the use of psychological tests* (Kendall, Jenkinson, de Lemos, & Clancy, 1994) is obtainable from: The Australian a　the administration of drugs (including alcohol and caffeine);

b　contact with any potentially harmful items or substances;

c　the use of invasive procedures (e.g., the taking of samples or the introduction of electrodes);

d　doubt about the participant's capacity to give consent to take part in the investigation (for example, in studies of young children, or the mentally handicapped);

e　the participant is suffering, or potentially suffering, distress or anxiety or physical discomfort;

f　the use of children as participants where the experiment falls outside the usual range of experiments in perception, memory, everyday skills, etc;

g　deception—with regard to what will happen during the investigation, to the real purpose of the investigation, or to the basis on which the participants are selected;

h　the use of patients under medical supervisions as participants, who may be particularly sensitive to the procedures employed;

i　asking participants sensitive questions that encroach on their privacy to a degree that might be considered by the participants as offensive or stressful to answer (e.g., questions about sexual preferences or political convictions).

APPENDIX 4.5. GUIDELINES FOR MEDICAL RESEARCH

A further set of guidelines, directed towards medical investigators, is the Medical Research Council's *Responsibility in Investigations on Human Participants and Material on Personal Information* (1992). This is obtainable from the Medical Research Council, 20 Park Crescent, London W1N 4AL. These guidelines should be consulted if you are doing a study involving any kind of medical intervention, and/or the use of patients.

Psychological Society Inc., PO Box 126, Carlton South 3053, Victoria, Australia.

This code includes a very detailed supplement on the use of psychological tests, drawing on the codes of both the American Psychological Association and the British Psychological Society as well as other sources. The guidelines are geared towards the needs of users employing psychological tests for assessment and guidance rather than research, but many of the provisions are important in research as well as assessment.

This part of the Appendix covers some general relevant features of the code, and Appendices 5.2 and 4.3 cover more specific features.

The code covers the professional conduct of psychologists in the following areas:

- general principles of conduct including responsibility, competence, and propriety
- assessment procedures
- consulting relationships
- teaching of psychology
- supervision and training
- research
- public statements
- professional relationships.

The code offers more detailed guidelines in specific areas, including:

- client/psychologist physical contact
- psychological test interpretation and report writing.

The most relevant of these guidelines are on *assessment procedures*. The code of practice here includes the necessity for:

- appropriate assessments that are administered and interpreted accurately
- ensuring that assessments are reliable, valid, and not obsolete
- confidentiality
- assessments by appropriately trained and qualified people.

It is unlikely that your testing procedure calls for *physical contact*. This should be avoided, as should any other verbal or non-verbal behaviour that might be construed as invasive, or as a sexual approach.

APPENDIX 4.2. CONDUCTING AN INDIVIDUAL TESTING SESSION

The suggestions below are based on Kendall et al. (1994), the supplement to the Australian Psychological Society's *Code of Professional Conduct* (1994; see Appendix 4.1), on the use of psychological tests, obtainable from the Australian Psychological Society, see p. 114).

Those conducting testing sessions should:

- establish rapport, to minimise anxiety and maximise motivation
- practise test administration before doing "real" testing
- adhere strictly to instructions for administration, and to verbatim instructions
- watch for signs of stress, boredom, anxiety, or fatigue
- provide encouragement without revealing correctness or incorrectness, approval or disapproval of responses (unless this is called for as part of test administration).

APPENDIX 4.3. FEEDBACK

These suggestions for good practice with regard to the giving of feedback are based on Kendall et al. (1994; see Appendix 4.2), who provide a much fuller set of guidelines.

- When introducing the session, state that feedback will (or could) be given (if desired).
- State that tests of personality, attitude, mood, and the like depend on *self-report*, and therefore the results depend on how the person has chosen to respond.
- If and when results are given, they should be given as fully as possible, and without the use of evaluative and possibly damaging terms (e.g., "failure", "better", "worse").
- Feedback that may be damaging or offensive should not be given.

APPENDIX 4.4. ETHICAL COMMITTEE OF ROYAL HOLLOWAY UNIVERSITY OF LONDON: NOTES FOR GUIDANCE

The essentials of these guidelines (Royal Holloway University of London, 1988) appear in Chapters 2, 3, and 4. They are quoted more fully here.

1   The following are general principles to be followed by all investigators who carry out investigations involving human participants:
    a   participants should be told as much as possible about the investigation that they are being asked to take part in, and their explicit consent must be obtained;
    b   where deception is involved in any investigation, participants should be carefully debriefed, and the right of participants to withhold the data collected about them in such an investigation should be respected;
    c   the data obtained about a participant should be kept strictly confidential (and, if held on a computer, the use of those data should conform with the requirements of the Data Protection Act);
    d   the data collected in an investigation should not be used for purposes different from those originally specified without the participant's consent;
    e   it should be made clear to a participant that he or she may withdraw from the investigation at any time without giving a reason;
    f   the research should have clear intended benefit(s), which can be described at the outset.
2   The approval of the ethical committee must be obtained in advance for any investigations involving human participant which might give rise to ethical problems. Sections 3 and below give a guide to the kinds of investigations for which approval would normally be required.
3   It is not possible to specify in advance precisely what constitutes an investigation which might give rise to ethical problems. However, the committee would normally wish to see the details of proposed investigations which involve any of the following:

Reliability

Notes on statistics packages

The specific instructions for computing given in these appendices are for SPSS for Windows users. Full instructions are given for carrying out the necessary operations to enter and check data, and to compute and improve reliability.

SPSS for Windows is frequently updated. As I write, SPSS 10.0 is the most modern, but this will almost certainly not be the case by the time you read this. The changes made with each new edition of SPSS are improvements such as modifications to output format, the addition of new statistical tests, or modifications to the options for procedures. The general menus and output formats remain constant, except for a change in formatting in SPSS 7.5 and later versions. This means that these instructions should be appropriate for any later editions of SPSS.

Loewenthal (1996) gives instructions for calculating reliability, suitable for those with statistics software that has no reliability facility, for those without a computer, and for those using older statistics packages (SPSS-X, SPSS-PC, CSS).

For further details of statistics packages and their suppliers, consult the CTI web site (see p. 163). This web site has a useful search engine. Other statistics packages for reliability analysis include:

- SYSTAT
- SAS/STAT
- Silver and Hittner (1998) describe some software for specialised forms of reliability analysis.

APPENDIX 5.1. TYPES OF DATA, CODING, AND STATISTICS

You need to be aware what kind of number-scale you are using when you code your data. The type of number-scale will affect the choice of statistics that are appropriate. Consult the guide below (and, if necessary, Chapter 5), or consult a suitable book (such as Coolican, 1999; de Vaus, 1993; Gravetter & Wallnau, 1999) or an appropriate person if you feel unsure on any of the points.

Interval data

Age and other numerical data (such as number of children, years of education, and the like) can be entered straight onto the computer. It is called interval data because you know the size of the interval between two numbers—the difference between 3 and 2 is the same as the difference between 2 and 1. If this sounds like a strange thing to be concerned about, be assured that it *is* important. It is quite likely that some of the data you deal with will not be interval data: Other types of data are described later, and in Table A5.1. Interval data is suitable for *parametric* statistical analysis including anova, Pearson correlation, *t*-test, multiple regression analysis.

Ordered (or ordinal) data

Here the data may look like numerical data, but there is a difference. With ordinal data you can only be sure that one number is greater than another, but you cannot be sure by how much. Supposing I rank three brands of chocolate in order of preference, with brand X first (rank = 1), brand Y second (rank = 2), and brand Z third (rank = 3). We know that 1, 2, and 3 are in order of magnitude, but we do not know anything about the *size* of the intervals between them. I might like brand X very much, much better than brand Y. However, brand Y is only a bit nicer than brand Z, but this is not reflected in rank-order data. Ordinal data may be used in *non-parametric* statistics, suitable for ordinal data, such as Mann-Whitney U, Kendall's Tau, Kruskal-Wallis one-way anova, and Jonkheere's Trend Test. In some cases it may be useful to treat the data as categorical, particularly as dichotomous (see later), but never treat it as interval data. Taking the most likely scenarios, you can use ordinal data in the non-parametric tests of

Table A5.1   Different types of number scale: Interval, ordinal, and nominal

	Sample data from one participant	Interval	Ordinal	Nominal
	Type of snack	Rating for nutrition (1–7)*	Order of preference	Taste (sweet=1, spicy=2, bland=3)
	Chocolate	7	5	1
	Pizza	4	3	2
	Crisps	4	4	2
	Nuts	1	1	3
	Muesli-bar	2	2	1
Descriptive statistics	–	Range, Means, Standard Deviations	Range, Medians	Frequencies, Cross-tabs
Inferential statistics		Parametric: e.g., anova, t-test, Pearson correlation, Multiple regression	Non-parametric for ordinal data: e.g., Kruskal-Wallis, anova, Spearman correlation	Non-parametric for nominal data e.g., chi-square, loglinear analysis

* Treating a 7-point rating scale as an interval scale assumes that the intervals are "equal-appearing", as discussed in Chapter 1, and in Appendix 5.1.

association just listed. Ordinal data may also be used in cross-tabs and chi-squares, though you may have to collapse some categories to get a result that can be interpreted. Ordinal data should not be used in tests suitable only for parametric data, such as anova, or most other forms of multivariate analysis.

Nominal (or categorical) data

Here, you do not even know that one number is greater or less than another number. Numbers are just used to indicate *category differences.* In Table A5.1. there are three categories for food taste: mainly sweet, mainly spicy, and bland. If you are going to code these, you should represent them by numbers (because computer statistical packages do not like and cannot normally use alphabetical data). You can see that the numbers 1, 2, and 3 are not ordered. It can be *very* advantageous to have just *two* categories, rather than more than two. This is called *dichotomous* data. Statistics and interpretation become much clearer and simpler, and important statistics are possible with dichotomous data. Notably, statistics packages *can* run correlations and reliability statistics on dichotomous data. The techniques are called, respectively, point biserial correlation, and the Kuder-Richardson KR-20 reliability coefficient. It is also allowable to include variables involving dichotomous data as independent variables in a multiple regression analysis. Unlike categorical data with more than two categories, dichotomous data are ordered. The moral of all this is to try and reduce categorical data to dichotomies, where it is sensible to do so. You do not have to do this when you code the data; you can make lots of categories and then collapse them into two when you are computing (see the instructions for recoding in Appendix section 5.3).

Rating scales

What about ratings? Are they interval or ordinal scales? If I rate my liking for chocolate on a 5-point scale, and brand X gets a 5, brand Y gets a 4, and brand Z gets a 3, is the difference between the 5 and the 4 the same as the difference between the 4 and the 3? Generally *rating scales may be treated as interval scales,* unless you suspect the contrary. Likert (1932) suggested this when he developed his best-selling method of scale construction involving rating. Likert's suggestion was that the intervals in such rating scales should be *equal-appearing.*

APPENDIX 5.2. AN EXAMPLE OF CODING

Figure A5.1 illustrates a simple coding scheme for the beginning of the questionnaire shown in Figure 3.2; lots of others could have been devised. The answers to the "test" part of the questionnaire (the questions on prayer, in the example) do not need any special

QUESTIONNAIRE ON PRAYER

We are studying people's views on the uses of prayer.
Your answers to the following questions would be very helpful. Your answers will be confidential and anonymous, identified only by a code number. You need not answer any questions that you would prefer to leave unanswered.

Thank you.

Date _____ **(do not code)**
Your age _____ **(enter as given)**
Male/Female _____ **(1=male, 0=female)**
Current marital status (Circle one): **(code 1 if currently in stable relationship: married, engaged or cohabiting, 0 otherwise)**
   married **(1)**
   engaged **(1)**
   single **(0)**
   cohabiting **(1)**
   divorced **(0)**
   widowed **(0)**
   separated **(0)**
Number of children, if any _____ **(enter as given)**
Their ages _____ **(code 1 if any under 18, 0 otherwise)**
Your occupation _____ **(code 1 if earning, 0 otherwise)**
If married, your spouse's occupation _____ **(code 1 if earning, 0 otherwise)**
Do you regard yourself as spiritual? _____ **(Yes=1, No=0)**
Do you belong to any church, mosque, or synagogue? _____ **(Yes=1, No=0)**
How often do you attend? (Circle one)
   daily **(4)**
   weekly **(3)**
   monthly **(2)**
   occasionally **(1)**
   never **(0)**
How often do you pray? (Circle one)
   daily **(4)**
   weekly **(3)**
   monthly **(2)**
   occasionally **(1)**
   never **(0)**
How often do you study religious texts? (Circle one)
   daily **(4)**
   weekly **(3)**
   monthly **(2)**
   occasionally **(1)**
   never **(0)**

Figure A5.1   Sample questionnaire, with codings.

coding. They can be entered onto the computer database just as they were given. Most of the answers to the first part of the questionnaire, which deals with background (social-demographic) information, need to be coded before they can be entered onto the computer. I have suggested coding in which some variables such as marital status, details of children, occupation, and religious membership have been reduced to simple 0/1 dichotomies, to make statistics more straightforward, but you may wish to use a more elaborate categorisation and reduce it later. If you do use a more elaborate categorisation, look in Appendix 5.3 for instructions on how to recode.

Figure A5.2 shows the answers, and their coded versions, of a hypothetical participant on this first part of the questionnaire.

APPENDIX 5.3. MAKING AND CHECKING A DATABASE IN SPSS FOR WINDOWS

Entering data

To enter data in SPSS for Windows, follow these steps.

1 *Enter SPSS*—click on Start/Programs/SPSS for Windows, or other method of entry as advised by your computing adviser. An empty data-entry spreadsheet should appear, with the highlight in the top left-hand cell. The highlight can be moved to this position by pressing CTRL + HOME simultaneously.

2 *Type in the data.* What you type will appear in a small dialogue box above the spreadsheet itself, and just under the menu bars. Any errors made in this dialogue box can be easily corrected using the method you prefer—the DELETE keys for small errors, or highlight and re-type for longer pieces of material. Press ENTER (◄—) to put each piece of data in the highlighted cell. It is usually easiest to type in the data moving horizontally across the spreadsheet. Enter the participant's ID number in the left-hand cell of each horizontal line, and then use the right-arrow key to move to each new cell. Move to a new line for each new case (participant). It is important to let each *row* contain the data for each participant, and each *column* to contain the data for each variable. This is important because that is the way SPSS will read the information when it does any statistics.

```
ID 1
Your age 22
Male/Female male (1)
Current marital status (underline one):
   married
   engaged
   single (0)
   cohabiting
   divorced
   widowed
   separated
Number of children, if any 0
Their ages – (0)
Your occupation student (0)
If married, your spouse's occupation –
Do you regard yourself as spiritual? Yes (1)
Do you belong to any church, mosque, or synagogue? No (0)
How often do you attend? (Underline one)
   daily
   weekly
   monthly
   occasionally (0)
   never
How often do you pray? (Underline one)
   daily
   weekly
   monthly
   occasionally
   never (0)
How often do you study religious texts? (Underline one)
   daily
   weekly
   monthly
   occasionally (1)
   never
```

Figure A5.2   Sample coding

3   *Missing data*: Just leave the relevant cell(s) empty. A single full-stop point (.) should appear in any cell with missing data.

4   *Correcting data*: Move the highlight to the cell needing correction, type in the correct entry, and press the ENTER (↵) key.

5   *To copy or move* sections of data: Use click/drag to highlight the section to be moved. Select Edit, and click on Copy or Cut (as appropriate). Move the cursor to the cell where the section is to be pasted, and click. Select Edit/Paste.

6 *Name variables*: When you have entered your data (or before you have finished, if you wish), enter names for variables. Each column contains data for each variable: move the highlight to any cell in the column, select Data/Define variable, click, type the variable name in the top (highlighted cell of the) dialogue box which appears, and press ENTER (↵). You can change the variable names at any time, using this same method. SPSS 10.0 will involve doing this (and changing the value labels as described in the next paragraph) through a Variable View window.

7 *Value labels*: If you wish, you can use the "Change Settings" area in the dialogue box to define the variable: give a full description of the variable, and the value labels. Click on "Change setting", then "Labels". For example, under "Variable label" you could describe the variable "married" as "whether now-married or not". Under "Value labels", you can record that now-married = 1, not-now-married = 0, as follows:

- enter "1" under "value"
- type "now-married" by "value label"
- click on "Add"
- enter "0" under "value"
- type "not-now-married" by "value label"
- click on "Add"
- click on "Continue"
- click on "OK".

It is useful to record these value labels if you are working on a database that is going to be used and re-used a few times. Sometimes the value labels will appear on the database, rather than the values themselves. Thus, you might see words like "Male" and "Female" in the data cells, rather than numbers. SPSS will still perform statistics on the numbers themselves. You may want to change the entries from the value labels to the values themselves (or vice versa). Click on the little icon that looks like a luggage label. On the toolbar, it should be the second from the end, on the right.

8 *Recoding*. There are two reasons why you might need to do some recoding at this point. First, when you have *reverse-meaning* items, for example "I hate chocolate" on a scale assessing liking for chocolate, or "Prayer is a waste of time" on a scale measuring the perceived usefulness of prayer. There are good reasons for including some items like this, as described in

Chapter 3. Second, when you have a categorical variable with lots of values, and for reasons described in Chapter 5 and in Appendix section 5.1 above, you decide it would helpful to *recode it as a dichotomous variable*. To *recode reverse-meaning items*, use the *recode into same variables* option:

- Select Transform/Recode/Into Same Variables.
- Select the variables to be recoded (e.g., item 4, item 6) and move them into the "Numeric Variables" box on the right, by clicking on the right-pointing arrow-head.
- Click on Old and New Values.
- Suppose your participants had been asked to rate how much they agree with each statement on a scale from 1 to 5, where 5 means strong agreement, and 1 means strong disagreement. For the reverse-meaning items, you will need to change all the 5s into 1s, all the 4s into 2s, all the 2s into 4s, and all the 1s into 5s; 3, the mid-point, stays as it is. So, in the Old and New Values screen:
  - enter 5 into the Old Values box
  - enter 1 into the New Values Box
  - click on Add. 5→1 should appear in the box headed Old→New.
  - repeat these three steps for 4→2, 2→4, and 1→5. (Remember, it is very important to enter *all* the reverse-scoring for the variables concerned on the one occasion, and remember that changing "5" to "1", or "2" to "−2" does just that (for the variables you have selected). It does *not* change "1" to "5", or "−2" to "2").
  - click on Continue
  - click on OK.

A similar procedure is followed for *recoding categorical variables with many values into dichotomous variables*, except that here it is safer to *recode into a new (different) variable*, so that you retain the original information for possible future use. So, to recode into a dichotomy:

- Select Transform/Recode/Into Different Variables.
- Select the variables to be recoded (e.g., relgroup) and move them into the "Numeric Variables→Output Variables" box on the right, by clicking on the right-pointing arrowhead.
- Now you must give a name to the new (output) variable(s). Type a suitable name into the Output Variable Name box.

For example, Relgroup was coded as 0 if no campus group was joined, and 1 or 2 according to *which* campus religious group was joined. We now want to recode to a variable showing *whether* a campus religious group was joined at all. So the new variable could be called "joined", and all the religious groups concerned (only two in this case) can be recoded as "1", to represent the fact that the individuals concerned joined a religious group. Under "Label" you can enter a description of the new variable, such as "Whether joined campus religious group".

- Click on Old and New Values.
- If there is only one value to be changed, it can be entered individually, into the top box under "Old Value". However it may be quicker to use one of the "Range" options if there is a longish string of consecutive numbers to be changed. In the example under consideration, you just need to change "2" into "1", so just enter 2 into the top box.
- Enter "1" in the New Value box.
- Because you are recoding into a new variable, you also have to tell SPSS to copy all the old values that are remaining unchanged. So enter 0 into the Old Value box, select Copy Old Value/Add. Enter other unchanged values in the same way. If there are any missing values in the variable, select System Missing under Old Value, and Copy Old Value followed by Add, under New Value.
- Click on Continue.
- Click on OK.

9   *Save data*: Select File/Save As. A Save As Data File dialogue box will appear. Type in the filename e.g., religion.sav. If you want to save on a floppy disc, click on (A:) in the field headed Save In. Otherwise select an appropriate directory. In the bottom of the dialogue box, are options for the format to be used. Normally the default will be SPSS *.sav. This saves the data in SPSS for Windows format. Note that .SAV is used automatically when naming and saving data files in SPSS for Windows, but if you are using an older version of SPSS for Windows you may have to name this filename extension yourself.

10   *To retrieve data*: Select File/Open Data. A dialogue box will appear. Either: Type in the filename (e.g., a:prayer.sav), or click on the little down-pointing arrow to the right of the Look

In box. This will display a choice of drives or directories. Double-click on (A:) (or the appropriate drive, and then if necessary the appropriate directory) in the Look In box. All files on your floppy disc ending in .SAV will be listed. Select the file to be retrieved and click. Check that the filename in the Name box is indeed the file you want, select OK and click. The data file may now be edited (or analysed).

Checking the database

Before starting statistical analysis, you should carry out the following checks for accuracy. I have described three checks, starting with the quickest and easiest, but if you carry out the second check, there is no real need for the first, and if you carry out the third check, there is no real need for the first two. If you have labelled your values, and these labels are showing up, rather than the numbers you need to check, place the cursor anywhere in the column concerned, and click on the little icon that looks like a luggage label, near the end on the right.

First, a *preliminary scan ("eye-balling")*. This may only enable you to detect errors which would be detected anyway, in the second and third checks. But it is always a good idea to "eyeball" your data. It is embarrassing to find out—when it is too late to do anything about it—that there are errors that could have been detected if you had just glanced over your material. So—glance over your database. It is usually easier to do this if the database has been printed out. *To print*, with the database on the screen, either click the Print icon (it looks like a printer), or select File, then Print. Look quickly over the database for things that should not be there, for example ages like 3025, or values like 53, when you should have typed "30" and "25", "5" and "3" in separate cells. Note any errors, and check your original data for the correct entry. Then go back to the computer database and correct the entries. *To correct errors* on the computer database, move the cursor to the cell concerned, and type in the correct entry. This will not appear in the cell itself, but in the dialogue box immediately under the tool bars. When you press ENTER (◄—), the corrected entry should then appear in the highlighted cell. *Save* the new, corrected version of the database, including at least one back-up copy.

The second check of the database involves asking for frequencies of each variable, and scanning the results. This may show up entries that have no business being there, but which do not stand out visually, so you might not have spotted them on the first check. Examples would be an age like 16 (when all your participants were over 18), or a rating of 6 on a scale ranging from 1 to 5. To obtain frequencies in SPSS:

- with the database on the screen, select Statistics (Analyse in some versions of SPSS)
- select Summarise (Descriptives in some versions of SPSS), then Frequencies
- move *all* variables into the Variables box, then click on OK.

Scan for unlikely or impossible values, such as ages like 2 or 99 when all participants were aged 18–60, or values like 0, 6, 25, or 3.341 on a rating scale involving only the whole numbers from 1 to 5. Locate all errors on the database—this is easier to do on a paper database. You should then look at your original records, note the correct entry, and when all corrections have been made on the paper database, amend the computer database as described previously, and save. Some sample outputs are shown in Table A5.2. You might like to look at them to see if you can spot possible errors. (The "answers" to the error-spotting exercise in Table A5.2 are: Age has two values of 2, and one of 451. These would need to be located and corrected. Religious affiliation has one value of 12, and Q1 has one value of 0 and one of 11.)

The third method of checking the database will uncover any errors that cannot be detected using the first and second methods—for example, entering 2 when 3 should have been entered, for a rating on a 1 to 5 scale. This third method is best done working in a pair. One member of the pair looks at the original data, and the other at a printout of the database. One person reads out their data, and the other calls out when they spot a mis-match. Correct all errors on the paper print-out, then correct the electronic version, save it and back it up. As stated, if you are able to carry out this type of check (and ideally, you should), then the first two checks are not strictly necessary.

Replacing missing data

Before starting reliability analysis, you might need to give some thought to the question of missing data. Some people may not have

Table A5.2 Locating errors from SPSS frequency data: Age, Religiously affiliated, and Prayer1

Age		Freq	Percent	Valid Percent	Cumulative Percent
Valid	2.00	2	2.0	2.0	2.0
	18.00	4	4.0	4.0	6.0
	19.00	4	4.0	4.0	10.0
	20.00	2	2.0	2.0	12.0
	21.00	2	2.0	2.0	14.0
	22.00	6	6.0	6.0	20.0
	23.00	10	10.0	10.0	30.0
	27.00	2	2.0	2.0	32.0
	28.00	2	2.0	2.0	34.0
	29.00	10	10.0	10.0	44.0
	31.00	1	1.0	1.0	45.0
	33.00	3	3.0	3.0	48.0
	34.00	15	15.0	15.0	63.0
	35.00	10	10.0	10.0	73.0
	36.00	1	1.0	1.0	74.0
	37.00	1	1.0	1.0	75.0
	38.00	1	1.0	1.0	76.0
	39.00	1	1.0	1.0	77.0
	40.00	1	1.0	1.0	78.0
	42.00	2	2.0	2.0	80.0
	45.00	6	6.0	6.0	86.0
	46.00	2	2.0	2.0	88.0
	53.00	1	1.0	1.0	89.0
	55.00	1	1.0	1.0	90.0
	56.00	7	7.0	7.0	97.0
	57.00	1	1.0	1.0	98.0
	59.00	1	1.0	1.0	99.0
	451.00	1	1.0	1.0	100.0
	Total	100	100.0	100.0	
Total	100	100.0			

RELAFFIL (whether religiously affiliated=1, or not=0):

		Freq	Percent	Valid Percent	Cumulative Percent
Valid	0.00	40	40.0	40.0	40.0
	1.00	59	59.0	59.0	99.0
	12.00	1	1.0	1.0	100.0
	Total	100	100.0	100.0	
Total	100	100.0			

continues overleaf

Table A5.2   (cont.)

Q1 (ratings of 1–5):

		Freq	Percent	Valid Percent	Cumulative Percent
Valid	0.00	1	1.0	1.0	1.0
	2.00	19	19.0	19.2	20.2
	3.00	30	30.0	30.3	50.5
	4.00	28	28.0	28.3	78.8
	5.00	20	20.0	20.2	99.0
	11.00	1	1.0	1.0	100.0
	Total	99	99.0	100.0	
Missing	System Missing	1	1.0		
	Total	1	1.0		
Total		100	100.0		

answered all questions, and missing data can be a nuisance because SPSS normally excludes *all* cases with even *one* piece of missing data from just *one* of the variables included in any analysis. Here are some suggestions to consider:

• If there are very few pieces of missing data, you may ignore the "problem". Some information will obviously not be used in all analyses, but if this involves just one or two cases this may be a trivial loss.

• If you find that much of the missing information is from *one* (or two, or a few) variables only, you may be able to exclude that variable from the analysis. For example if only 60% of participants answered one of the items on a scale, but all other items had been answered by nearly everyone, it would be advisable to exclude that item from the scale. There is certainly something suspicious about an item that nearly half the participants would not or could not answer, and you might want to look at it to see if you can work out why. Almost certainly it should not be included in further work. On the other hand, there might be a variable like age or religion for which some people have not given any information. You can still use the information that has been given in some analyses, for example in offering descriptive statistics for the sample. Remember to indicate how many (or what proportion) of people did not give this piece of information.

- In some circumstances, it may be acceptable to replace missing values, with made-up values. This should only be done if it would make sense to replace missing values in this way. The commonest replacement strategy is to replace missing values with the mean for that variable. This would *not* make sense for variables like age, or religious affiliation. It might make sense if you have say, 30 participants who have each left out one answer, each to a different item on a scale. If you have only 100 participants, you will lose a large amount of data from your analyses, and you might try replacing missing values with the mean on the variable concerned. To do this in SPSS:
- select Transform
- select Replace Missing Values
- select the variables which have missing values which you want to replace; move them, by clicking on the right-pointing arrow-head, into the New Variables box
- the default option is replace missing values with the series mean (mean for that variable)
- click on OK
- SPSS will put a new variable in your database, identifying it by a suffix of the form "_1"
- you can try analyses using these new variables, instead of the old ones with missing values—if you do this, remember to report that you replaced missing values with series means, identifying the variables for which you did this.

It is not, however, very good practice to use items with replaced missing values in a reliability analysis. It is better to use the original data, warts and all. But there may be some analyses that you carry out later—in which you might want to compare total scores on your scale with other factors—in which the replacement of missing values is defensible.

APPENDIX 5.4. RELIABILITY ANALYSIS IN SPSS FOR WINDOWS

This Appendix section describes the steps needed to compute Cronbach's alpha (a coefficient of internal consistency) using SPSS for Windows.

Table A5.3 SPSS reliability
analysis output

Reliability coefficients
No of cases = 100
No of items = 8
Alpha = .6111

- Retrieve your data if necessary. Select File/Open/Data. Type the filename in the dialogue box (e.g., a:prayer.sav), or select the appropriate drive, directory, and file, and click on OK.
- Select Analyse (Statistics in some versions of SPSS)/Scale/ Reliability Analysis.
- Enter all items in your scale (or subscale) into the [items] box. Select from the box on the left, click, and click on the right-pointing arrow. This will enter the selected items into the [items] box.
- Select required model. Normally, the default option, Alpha, should be used.
- Select OK.

A sample output is shown in Table A5.3. Table A5.3 is not difficult to interpret. It first tells you how many cases were included in the analysis, and how many items. Check that you are happy with the number of cases included in the analysis. If there are many missing, check for missing data and consider the suggestions made earlier, for dealing with missing data. Then check that the right number of items are there, i.e., the number you intended to include. If that is wrong, you need to go back to the items box in the reliability analysis (just select Analyse/Scale/Reliability Analysis again). Check and rectify the contents. Finally, the statistic you have been working so hard for, Alpha. In Table A5.3 it is not particularly high—as discussed in Chapter 5, 0.8 and above is good, and 0.7 and above is satisfactory, 0.6111 is not very satisfactory, but it is not hopeless. If you have a result like this, you could turn to the next section (5.5) and follow the steps described to improve alpha.

This appendix section has not dealt with reliability indices other than Cronbach's alpha. If you have reason to believe that split-half reliability, Guttman coefficients or other options would be in order, these can be computed by altering the model in the Model box in the lower left of the Reliability Analysis window.

APPENDIX 5.5. IMPROVING RELIABILITY

Reliability is improved by looking at the item-total correlations of each item, and rejecting those with low item-total correlations. Alternatively, SPSS will tell you the effect on alpha, of rejecting any given item from the scale. In practice, it makes no difference whether you are guided by the item-total correlation information, or by the information about the effect on alpha. To obtain these pieces of information:

- select Analyse/Scale/Reliability
- move the items in the scale into the Items box, as described earlier (if they are not already there)
- click on Statistics, in the lower right corner of the Reliability Analysis window
- a new window will appear. Select Scale if item deleted—click on the adjacent box and a tick (check) should appear
- continue
- OK.

A sample output is shown in Table A5.4. Look at the column headed "corrected item-total correlation". This tells you how well

Table A5.4   SPSS reliability analysis output: Item-total statistics

	Scale mean if item deleted	Scale variance if item deleted	Corrected item-total correlation	Alpha if item deleted
Q1	21.5000	30.3535	.4611	.5521
Q2	21.8000	28.1414	.5735	.5168
Q3	22.1000	31.0000	.6576	.5436
Q4	21.9000	31.4444	.4047	.5674
Q5	22.0000	29.1515	.5285	.5328
Q6	22.2000	33.4545	.1341	.6200
Q7	22.0000	29.6970	.6268	.5286
Q8	21.5000	23.6869	.1026	.8109

Reliability coefficients
No of cases = 100.0
No of items = 8
Alpha = .6111

Table A5.5   SPSS reliability analysis output after removing selected items

	Scale mean if item deleted	Scale variance if item deleted	Corrected item-total correlation	Alpha if item deleted
Q1	15.2000	14.9091	.6604	.8486
Q2	15.5000	13.5859	.7248	.8383
Q3	15.8000	16.1212	.8153	.8349
Q4	15.6000	15.3939	.6625	.8481
Q5	15.7000	15.3636	.5384	.8728
Q7	15.7000	15.3636	.7167	.8399

Reliability coefficients
No of cases = 100.0
No of items = 6
Alpha = .8693

the item correlates with the others. If you look in the output for Table A5.4, you see that the lowest item-total correlations are for items 6 and 8. Item 8 should certainly go, and we might consider throwing out 6. Correlations of the order of .15 or less could definitely mean the death sentence for any item, unless you are desperately short of higher correlations. The column headed "alpha if item deleted" tells you what the alpha coefficient would be if that item were got rid of. As you can see, the effect of throwing out the less cohesive items is to raise alpha, and vice versa. The first two columns tell you what would happen to the scale mean and variance if each item were deleted.

You can "throw out" items with unsatisfactory item-total correlations, and finish your computing as follows:

- Analyse/Scale/Reliability analysis.
- If all items are in the Items box (they will be if you are doing all the computing in one session), select the items you wish to discard (e.g., Q8, Q6), click on the left-pointing arrowhead.
- If no items are in the Items box, select those you wish to include (e.g., Q1–5,Q7), and click on the right-pointing arrowhead.
- OK.

A sample output is shown in Table A5.5. If alpha is now satisfactory, you can ignore the rest of the output. Table A5.5 shows an alpha well over 0.8, which is satisfactory. If alpha were still low, you should look at the "Alpha if item deleted" to see if there is scope for any further improvement. If any of the alphas in this column are higher than the alpha at the bottom of the output, then you could try removing the relevant item(s). However if the alphas in the left-hand column are all lower than the alpha at the bottom of the output—this is the case in Table A5.5—then there are no further improvements possible. At least, not in terms of removing items and recomputing alpha. Some suggestions are made in Chapter 5, for procedures to be followed if reliability coefficients are unsatisfactory.

If alpha is satisfactory: Compute statistics for the scale

- Select Analyse/Scale/Reliability Analysis.
- With the final selection of "good" items in the Items box, click on Statistics.
- (You can remove the tick/check from Scale if item deleted.)
- Tick/check Descriptives for Scale.
- Continue.
- OK.

A sample output is shown in Table A5.6. These statistics tell you the scale mean, variance, standard deviation, and number of items (variables) in the scale. This information should be given in any description of the scale.

If you wish, you can ask for *item means*. Select Analyse/Scale/ Reliability Analysis/Statistics/Descriptives for Item. The advantage of this is that if you (or anyone else using your scale) vary the number of items in the scale, comparisons with the item mean would still make some sense.

Table A5.6 Scale statistics: SPSS output after removing selected items (extract)

Mean	Variance	SD	No of variables
18.7000	21.2222	4.6068	6

APPENDIX 5.6. FACTOR AND PRINCIPAL COMPONENTS ANALYSES IN SPSS FOR WINDOWS

This part of Appendix 5 gives a very brief introduction to the use of factor and principal components analysis. This might be considered if you have failed to obtain a satisfactory coefficient of reliability, and you are wondering if there might be two or more subscales embedded in your measure. Factor or principal components analyses could identify such subscales. They would emerge as factors (or components) accounting for a reasonable proportion of variance, and on which several of your items would have high loadings.

Factor analysis is a method of examining associations between associations. It finds a small number of underlying dimensions from a larger number of variables, by consolidating the variance. In the case of a test or scale, it will enable your group items that seem to be assessing the same "factor", by examining the "loading" of all items on each factor, and selecting those with high loadings.

Factor analysis proceeds by first extracting factors, and then if more than one factor emerges, a rotation is carried out to give a clearer picture. Principal components analysis is not actually factor analysis, but it usually gives similar answers and is often used instead of factor analysis. Our illustrations will follow this option. We will use a popular method of rotation called varimax. Note that you are supposed to have at least three times as many participants as variables to get a meaningful result from factor or principal components analysis, so our little hypothetical example, with 100 participants and eight variables (items), does qualify.

- Select Analyse/Data Reduction/Factor. A Factor Analysis dialogue box will appear.
- Enter all items in your scale into the [variables] box. Select from the box on the left, click, and click on the right-pointing arrow. This will enter the selected items into the [variables] box.
- (A principal components analysis will be carried out by default. If for any reason you prefer another option, select this by clicking on Extraction. Tabachnick and Fidell (1996) or some other authoritative source would guide on the selection of another extraction method.)

- It is advisable to choose a rotation method, and varimax is the most commonly used method. If you wish for more discussion on rotation methods, consult Tabachnick and Fidell, or other suitable authority. You can choose a varimax rotation by clicking on Rotation, then Varimax.
- Continue.
- OK.

Part of a sample output is shown in Table A5.7. There will be more in the output, and Tabachnick and Fidell (1996), or (more simply) West (1991), or other suitable statistics book, for guidance on how to interpret and use this information. For the present, just concentrate on the bits headed Total Variance Explained, and Component Matrix.

Note that eight components (factors) have been extracted. Principal Components Analysis extracts as many components as there are variables, so if you had a measure with 50 items, 50 components would be extracted. Most of these will account for very little variance, and the eigenvalue is a guide to which components are important and which can be ignored. The *eigenvalue* of a factor or principal component indicates how much variance (in the original variables) is accounted for. One convention is to discount factors or principal components with eigenvalues of less than one. This is what has happened in the first part of Table A5.7. Eight components have been extracted (there were eight variables), but only three have eigenvalues greater than one, so the rest of the output concentrates on those. The upper part of Table A5.7 contains a repetition of information about the first (three) components, with further information about what happened to the variance explained after rotation. Table A5.7 tells us that the first factor (component) accounts for over 40% of the variance, and the first three factors between them account for nearly 80% of the variance. This means that these factors are important.

If there is more than one factor (with an eigenvalue greater than 1), then the factors should be rotated, and the component factor matrix reflects the result of this rotation. This matrix tells us how the different items on the questionnaire load on each factor (component). The loading is the correlation between that item and the factor. We can use this information to label the components (see later).

Table A5.7 SPSS factor and principal components analysis: Part of the output

Total variance explained

Component	Initial eigenvalues			Extraction sums of squared loadings			Rotation sums of squared loadings		
	Total	% of variance	Cumulative %	Total	% of variance	Cumulative %	Total	% of variance	Cumulative %
1	3.813	47.664	47.664	3.813	47.664	47.664	3.373	42.160	42.160
2	1.415	17.683	65.347	1.415	17.683	65.347	1.590	19.877	62.037
3	1.156	14.456	79.803	1.156	14.456	79.803	1.421	17.765	79.803
4	.877	10.956	90.759						
5	.474	5.927	96.686						
6	.159	1.993	98.679						
7	9.014E-02*	1.127	99.806						
8	1.551E-02	.194	100.000						

Component matrix

	Component		
	1	2	3
Q1	.787	.177	.412
Q2	.811	.100	−.141
Q3	.889	−8.214E-02	9.754E-02
Q4	.749	.623	4.245E-02
Q5	.678	−.278	.508
Q6	.164	.838	.321
Q7	.829	.433	−.187
Q8	.104	.100	.748

* Note: the notation E-02 indicates that there has been an overflow beyond the display capacity. In spite of appearances, the number (eigenvalue, in this case, and factor loading in the component matrix) is very small, and can be ignored.
Extraction Method: Principal Component Analysis. 3 components extracted in component matrix.

There will be more to the output than described, but hopefully enough is indicated of the important features of factor and principal components analysis.

Interpreting factor loadings and naming factors

The experts on factor analysis I have met turn a bit coy when it comes to talking about this bit. The awful truth is that after a massive amount of number-crunching (by SPSS), your job is to:

- look at which items have high loadings (above about 0.4) on each factor,
- decide what they have in common, and
- dream up a plausible name for each factor in the light of this.
- Factors which account for small amounts of variance may be dropped. (What constitutes "small" can vary somewhat, but this would normally be below about 8–10% of variance.)

Look at the items in the scale in relation to the loadings in the component (factor) matrix. For example, looking at the items in the hypothetical prayer scale, in relation to Table A5.7:

1 It is important to pray when you need help.
2 There are better routes to understanding life's mysteries than praying.
3 Praying gives comfort.
4 Regular contemplative prayer is important.
5 It is foolish to believe that prayers get answered.
6 People who get inspired by prayer are kidding themselves.
7 Prayer puts things in perspective.
8 Prayer is a waste of time

- All items except 6 and 8 loaded heavily on the first factor (component). We might suggest that this factor reflects general favourability towards prayer.
- Items 4, 6, and 7 loaded on the second factor. This factor might reflect a belief in the positive cognitive effects of prayer, particularly contemplative prayer. So we might label this second factor belief in the value of contemplative prayer.

- Items 1, 5 and 8 loaded heavily on the third factor. This factor looks as if it reflects belief in the instrumental uses of prayer.

You might run separate reliability analyses on any subscales identified in this way, but this is not strictly necessary. Factor or principal components analysis is normally considered sufficient evidence of the structure of scales and subscales.

Appendix to Chapter 6

Computation and validity

This appendix gives instructions for carrying out statistical tests for the main types of validity, using SPSS for Windows. Many of the tests are considered quite advanced, and instructions for their use and interpretation have been offered in as clear and simplified manner as possible. I hope that I have not over-simplified too greatly. More advice and information on the use of inferential statistics can be obtained from a suitably qualified person, or from a competent book such as Clark-Carter (1997), Cramer (1993), Field (2000), or Gravetter and Wallnau (1999).

APPENDIX 6.1. COMPUTING TOTAL SCORES ON YOUR MEASURE

Although you have by now obtained descriptive statistics (means, standard deviations, and other statistics) for your measure, using the SPSS reliability facility, this facility does not actually produce individual total scores for each participant. You will need to calculate these scores in order to do the necessary statistics to establish validity.

- Make sure SPSS is running (Start/Programs/SPSS), and that your database is opened (File/Open/Data, and then type in the filename, or select the appropriate drive and folder from the Look In menus, and click on the filename).
- Select Transform/Compute.
- In the top left dialogue box name the new variable you are going to compute, e.g., Total.

- Select the variables which are going to be computed, one at a time. Move each into the Numeric expression box (using the left-pointing arrowhead), with the appropriate operator which can either be typed in from the keyboard, or selected from the choice below the Numeric expression box. For example, if I wanted to compute the total score on the (hypothetical) reliable prayer scale, comprising items 1–5 and 7, my Numeric expression box should contain the expression: Q1 + Q2 + Q3 + Q4 + Q5 + Q7.
- OK.

A new variable, called (in this case) Total should appear in your database. You should save the new version of the database.

APPENDIX 6.2. CRITERION VALIDITY USING AN UNRELATED *T*-TEST

Here is how to use SPSS for Windows to examine the scores of two groups on your measure, for significant differences.
   First carry out the *t*-test:

- Select Analyse (Statistics)/Compare Means/Independent Samples *t*-test.
- For the Grouping Variable box, select the variable(s) you wish to use as independent variables. For example, if I wanted to see whether those who were religiously affiliated had higher scores on the prayer scale than those who are not affiliated, I would move the variable Relaffil into the grouping variables box.
- The grouping variable will have two question marks next to it. These are asking for the two values of that variable. Select Define Groups. Enter one value (e.g., 0) into the Group 1 box, and the other value (e.g., 1) into the Group 2 box. Obviously the grouping variable can only have two values, for a *t*-test to be appropriate. If it has three or more, you should be doing a one-way anova (see Appendix 6.5). If you can't remember what the values of your grouping variable are, you will have to abandon the *t*-test temporarily (click on the x in the top right corner, or on Cancel) and get back to your database to refresh your memory. Then start again at Select Analyse (Statistics).
- Continue.

- Now enter the dependent variable (e.g., Total) into the Test Variables box.
- OK.

A sample *t*-test output is shown in Table A6.1. The first part of the output is a table telling you what the mean scores (and standard deviations and errors) were for the two groups, on the prayer measure (called Total). The column to attend to is the one headed "mean". You can see that group 2's mean is higher that group 1's.

Was the difference statistically significant? What was the probability of observing those differences by chance? You can simply look at the row beginning "Equal variances assumed" for the *t* value and the significance level.

However, the traditional *t*-test (based on a pooled variance estimate) assumes homogeneity of variance, and the variance of the two groups may *not* be homogeneous. There are two ways to check this. First, and more simply, you can look at the variances (or standard deviations, which are the square root of the variances) to see if they are roughly similar. In the top part of Table A6.1, one group has a standard deviation that is nearly double that of the other group. These are clearly *not* similar. A second way of comparing the variances is offered in the first two columns of the SPSS output, which give the results of a test (Levene's) for homogeneity of variance. If the two groups have similar variances, the *F* ratio is small and the *p* value is *greater* than .05). Then, you may look for the *t* value based on a pooled variance estimate. If the two groups have non-homogeneous variance (i.e., they have significantly different variances, with a large *F* and a *p* of *less* than .05) then *t* needs to be based on separate variance estimates. So the rule is:

- if the first probability value is more than .05, look at the first *t*-value (pooled variance);
- if the first probability value is less than .05, look at the second *t*-value (separate variance).

In the previous example, the first probability value was less than .05, the variances of the two groups were non-homogeneous, and therefore the value of *t* in the lower row (21.81) should be taken. This second method of comparing variances can be unreliable, since it is said to be affected by sample size.

Table A6.1 SPSS t-test output

Group statistics

	Relaffil	No.	Mean	SD	SEM
TOTAL	.00	40	13.5250	2.2981	.3634
	1.00	60	22.1667	1.2236	.1580

Independent samples test
Levene's test for equality of variances

F 27.337
Sig. .000

t-test for equality of means

	t	df	Sig. (2-tailed)	Mean difference	SED	95% confidence interval of the mean	
						Lower	Upper
Equal variances assumed	−24.430	98	.000	−8.6417	.3537	−9.3436	−7.9397
Equal variances not assumed	−21.810	53.862	.000	−8.6417	.3962	−9.4361	−7.8473

SEM = standard error mean; SED = standard error difference.

Sometimes *t* appears with a minus sign, as in the previous example. You do not usually have to take account of this. It just indicates the direction of the difference between the groups, which is something you should have your eye on anyway. SPSS's convention is that *t* will have a minus sign if the second group has a higher mean than the first group. This is not a point to worry about, because there are easier ways to examine the direction of differences between groups. You can simply look at the means for each group, and see if the direction of differences makes sense. Thus in Table A6.1, it would be reasonable to expect the religiously affiliated to have a higher score on the prayer scale than those who are not affiliated, and this is in fact the case.

Although you do not have to worry about whether *t* is positive or negative, because there are easier ways to discover the direction of differences between groups, you may have to concern yourself with a related issue: the question of one- or two-tailed probabilities. To be honest, you should always be concerned about this! If you have predicted the *direction* of the difference between two groups, then you should take the *one-tailed* probability—assuming that you indeed observed a difference in the predicted direction. In the present case, the difference between the two groups was predicted, so a one-tailed probability should be used. This is got by dividing the quoted two-tailed probability by 2. In this example SPSS gives the two-tailed *p* as .000 (accurate to three decimal places), so the one-tailed *p* is still .000. If, for example, the two-tailed probability had been .05, the one-tailed probability would be .025. Obviously if the difference between two groups was in the direction opposite to that predicted, you would have to take the two-tailed probability. For some tests, SPSS allows you to specify whether you want one- or two-tailed probabilities, but this is not possible (at the time of writing) for the *t*-test.

APPENDIX 6.3. CONCURRENT VALIDITY: USING SPSS TO CALCULATE CORRELATIONS

Concurrent validity generally involves looking at the correlation between scores on your new scale and scores on a standard scale.

Table A6.2   SPSS correlation output

Correlations

	Standard	Total
Pearson correlation		
Standard	1.000	.554**
Total	.554**	1.000
Sig. (1-tailed)		
Standard		.000
Total	.000	
N		
Standard	100	100
Total	100	100

** Correlation is significant at the .01 level (1-tailed).

- Enter SPSS and open your data file.
- Analyse (Statistics)/Correlate/Bivariate.
- Select the variables to be correlated with each other. For example Total (participants' scores on your new, reliable measure) and Standard (scores on a standard measure of the same or similar factor). Move them into the Variables box, using the right-pointing arrowhead.
- Under Test of Significance, select One-tailed, assuming you have predicted the direction of the association between the two variables.
- OK.

A sample output is shown in Table A6.2. The upper part of the output tells you (twice over) the size of the correlation coefficient, and indicates the level of statistical significance. It tells you the names of the variables being correlated, the correlations with each other (this information is repeated, so just ignore the duplication) and the level of statistical significance. Here, a minus sign by the correlation means a *negative* association between the variables (high values on one go with low values on the other). Note that this output tells you one-tailed significance levels. With this output, if you had *not* predicted the direction of association (unlikely in the case of validity testing), you should ask for two-tailed tests of significance. The remainder of the output tells you the exact probability obtained, and the number of cases included in the analysis.

APPENDIX 6.4. CRITERION AND PREDICTIVE VALIDITY: ONE-WAY ANALYSIS OF VARIANCE IN SPSS, INCLUDING COMPARISONS BETWEEN GROUPS

If you are comparing *scores* on your measure with *scores* on some other measure, you should carry out correlations, as described earlier (Appendix 6.3). If, however, you are looking at scores on your measure in relation to "group membership" (a discontinuous, categorical variable, such as whether people belong to group A, B, or C, or performed behaviour X, Y, or Z), then you need to carry out either a *t*-test (see Appendix 6.1) or an analysis of variance (anova). A(n unrelated) *t*-test can be done when comparing scores of two groups, while anova is needed for more than two groups, and for more complex research designs outside the scope of this book.

As an aside, in terms of statistical theory, there is nothing really wrong with doing an anova to look for differences between scores of two groups, and the anova is just as "sensitive" as the *t*-test. They use the same information, in a very slightly different way.

To do a one-way anova in SPSS:

- Enter SPSS and open your data file.
- Select Analyse (Statistics)/Compare Means/One way ANOVA.
- Enter the dependent variable in the Dependent box (e.g., Total).
- Enter independent variable in the Factor box (e.g., Relgroup— in this example we are looking to see if there were differences between those who joined different campus religious groups, or who joined none, in their attitudes to prayer).
- Assuming you want to examine the comparison between each pair of groups for significant differences, click on the Post Hoc box, and select one of the options (normally LSD, Least Significant Differences).
- Continue.
- OK.

Sample outputs are shown in Table A6.3 and Table A6.4. To look at the relation between scores on the prayer measure, and religious-

Table A6.3 SPSS anova (one-way) output

Total	Sum of squares	df	Mean square	F	Sig.
Between groups	1875.615	2	937.807	431.176	.000
Within groups	210.975	97	2.175		
Total	2086.590	99			

Table A6.4 SPSS output for unplanned contrasts

(I) Relgroup	(J) Relgroup	Mean difference (I-J)	SE	Sig.	95% confidence interval	
					Lower bound	Upper bound
.00	1.00	-9.4750*	.330	.000	-10.1295	-8.8205
	2.00	-6.9750*	.404	.000	-7.7766	-6.1734
1.00	.00	9.4750*	.330	.000	8.8205	10.1295
	2.00	2.5000*	.404	.000	1.6984	3.3016
2.00	.00	6.9750*	.404	.000	6.1734	7.7766
	1.00	-2.5000*	.404	.000	-3.3016	-1.6984

*Multiple comparisons. Dependent variable: total. LSD (use Tukey's test if 4 or more levels of the independent variable). SE = standard error. *The mean difference is significant at the .05 level.

group-joining (Relgroup) we look at the row of figures at the Between Groups F ratio and significance level. In the example in Table A6.4, there is a very large F ratio and a very small (zero) significance level, indicating a very significant effect of group membership on attitudes to prayer. Did all three groups differ significantly from each other? The Multiple Comparisons table tells us that, yes, in this case, there were significant differences between *each* of the three groups, since there are significance levels well below .05 in the Significance column for each between-groups comparison.

In describing the results, you need to quote the between-groups F ratio and degrees of freedom, and the degrees of freedom for the residual variance (sometimes called the "error", in this case identical with the within-groups degrees of freedom)—in this case 97. The level of statistical significance should also be quoted. Thus, $F(2, 97) = 431.2$, $p < .001$. Group means should also be presented, and the significance of any comparisons between groups.

To present the results of an analysis of variance, you need to present an *analysis of variance table* if there was a fairly complex research design involving *two or more grouping variables*. The note at the end of this section mentions the command to be used in such a case) and/or a mixed analysis of variance involving within and between-subjects effects. In a case with only *one grouping variable*, an anova table is not necessary; you only need to focus on one F ratio, and the results can be presented by quoting the F ratio, the two relevant figures for degrees of freedom, and the probability. Thus, our example would be: Significant differences in prayer scores went with later religious-group-joining: $F(2, 97) = 431.18$, $p = .000$. The output will tell you the means associated with each group and enable you to see where the differences lie. These means should be quoted in presenting results.

Two-way analyses of variance

These may be done by selecting Analyse/General Linear Models/ Simple Factorial. The procedure is similar to that described previously, except that you enter two grouping (independent) variables in the Factor box, and define the ranges of both.

APPENDIX 6.5. CONFOUNDED VARIABLES: LOGLINEAR ANALYSIS, LOGISTIC REGRESSION, ANALYSIS OF COVARIANCE, AND MULTIPLE REGRESSION ANALYSIS

For more detailed discussion of these methods refer to a more advanced statistics text (Field, 2000; Tabachnick & Fidell, 1996), and/or the statistics software manual. This section simply gives SPSS commands and a very brief explanation for the output for each of these methods of analysis. Further options are available, and the manual should be consulted for details.

Note that Table 6.1 in Chapter 6 offers a brief guide as to when these analyses might be appropriate.

In all cases:

IV = independent (predictor) variable
DV = dependent (outcome) variable.

Loglinear analysis

Appropriate when the DV and all IVs (IV and covariates) are categorical. You can also do an n-dimensional chi-square, but oddly enough, although that is a simpler statistic in theory, it is quite complicated working out the order in which to enter the IVs in each "layer" of the analysis. It is also very exercising to interpret the contingency tables once you are using more than two or three IVs. I find that once I have got my head round them, it is to discover that there was a better order in which to layer the IVs. The instructions that follow are for a version of loglinear analysis that expresses the IV–DV relations in a relatively clear and simple form, and does not require you to take mind-stretching decisions about the order in which the IVs should be entered. (Acknowledgements to West, 1991, for drawing attention to this helpful variation of SPSS's loglinear analysis.)

- With SPSS running and your database in place, select Statistics (Analyse)/Loglinear/Model Selection.

- In the lower left corner of the Model Selection dialogue screen, select Options.
- Under Display for Saturated Model, select Association Tables.
- Continue.
- Enter the factors (variables) you wish to include, by highlighting them and using the right-pointing arrow to put them in the Factors box. The variables may be entered in any order. Remember that they should all be categorical variables.
- Two queries next to each variable will ask you to define the range of each variable. Select Define Range and enter the highest and lowest value of the variable concerned.
- Continue.
- OK.

As stated, SPSS offers several variations of loglinear analysis. The version described will give you, at the end of output, a section headed Tests of Partial Associations. This will show partial chi-squares and probabilities for associations between all combinations of variables. The association between the DV and each of the IVs will show you the "pure" relationship between the DV and the IV in question, with the effects of the other IVs partialled out.

Logistic regression

Appropriate when the DV is categorical, and the IVs (IV and covariates) are continuous. Logistic regression can also be used when some of the IVs are categorical.

- Select Analyse (Statistics)/Regression/Logistic.
- Enter the DV, which must be categorical, in the Dependent box.
- Enter the IVs in the Covariates box. These can be a mixture of categorical and continuous, though logistic regression is appropriate where most or all are categorical.
- The default method is Enter.
- OK.

The output is similar to that for multiple regression analysis. The last part of the output is the most crucial. It is headed Variables in the Equation, and it will include Betas and significance levels for the associations between each of the IVs and the DV. As conventional, significance levels of *less* than .05 may normally be taken as indicating a significant association between the DV, and the IV concerned.

Analysis of covariance

Appropriate when the IV is categorical, and the DV continuous. The covariates should preferably be continuous.

- Select Analyse (Statistics)/General Linear Model/Simple Factorial.
- Move the DV into the Dependent Variable box.
- Move the IV into the Factor(s) box, and define the range.
- Move the covariate(s) into the Covariate(s) box.
- Other boxes may be left empty.
- OK.

The output will express the "pure" effect of the IV on the DV (uncontaminated by the effects of the covariates), in the form of an *F* ratio (with its associated probability), in an anova table. The effect(s) of the covariates will also be shown in the anova table.

Multiple regression analysis

Appropriate when the DV is continuous, and the IVs (IV and covariates) are also continuous. However, a minority of categorical (dichotomous) IVs (covariates) can be included. SPSS offers several variations of multiple regression. The simplest is:

- Select Analyse/Regression/Linear.
- Enter DV into the Dependent box.
- Enter the IVs (IV and covariates) into the Independent(s) box.
- Normally the default Method (Enter) can be used.
- OK.

The final part of the output is the most crucial for interpreting the results. It is a table headed Coefficients. It includes Beta values for the IVs, expressing their relationship with the DV. The output also includes *t* values and probabilities, expressing the significance of the relationship between each of the IVs and the DV. These *t* values and significance levels can be looked at first, to see which—if any—variables related significantly to the DV.

Bibliography

Adorno, T.W., Frenkel-Brunswick, E., Levinson, D.J., & Sanford, R.N. (1950). *The authoritarian personality*. New York: Harper & Row.

Allport, G.W., & Vernon, P.E. (1960). *The study of values*. Boston: Houghton Mifflin.

American Educational Research Association, American Psychological Association, & National Council on Measurement in Education. (1985). *Standards for educational and psychological testing*. Washington, DC: Author.

American Psychiatric Association. (1980). *Diagnostic and statistical manual of mental disorders* (3rd rev. ed.). Washington, DC: Author.

Anastasi, A. (1988). *Psychological testing* (6th ed.). New York: Macmillan.

Anastasi, A., & Urbina, S. (1996). *Psychological testing* (7th ed.). Englewood Cliffs, NJ: Prentice Hall.

Arksey, H., & Knight, P.T. (1999). *Interviewing for social scientists: An introductory resource with examples*. London: Sage.

Arnkoff, D. (1983) Cognitive and specific factors in cognitive therapy. In M.J. Lambert (Ed.), *Psychotherapy and patient relationships*. Homewood, IL: Dow Jones-Irwin.

Australian Psychological Society Limited. (1994). *Code of professional conduct*. Victoria, Australia: Author.

Bartram, D. (1993). *Certificate of Competence in Occupational Testing (Level B): Discussion Paper*. Leicester, UK: British Psychological Society.

Bartram, D., & Lindley, P.A.A. (2000) *Psychological Testing: The BPS Level A Open Learning Programme* (2nd ed.). Leicester, UK: British Psychological Society Books.

Bartram, D., Lindley, P.A.A., Foster, J., & Marshall, L. (1990). *Review of psychometric tests for assessment in vocational training*. Leicester, UK: BPS Books.

Batson, C.D. (1976). Religion as prosocial: Agent or double agent? *Journal for the Scientific Study of Religion, 15,* 29–45.

Batson, C.D., Schoenrade, P., & Ventis, W.L. (1993). *Religion and the individual.* New York/Oxford, UK: Oxford University Press.

Beck, A.T., Rush, A.J., Shaw, B.F., & Emery, G. (1979). *Cognitive therapy and depression.* New York: Guilford Press.

Beck, A.T., & Steer, R.A. (1987). *The Beck Depression Inventory.* San Antonio, TX: The Psychological Corporation/Harcourt Brace Jovanovitch.

Bem, S. (1974). The measurement of psychological androgyny. *Journal of Consulting and Clinical Psychology, 42,* 155–162.

Bradley, C. (1998). *Inaugural professorial lecture.* Royal Holloway College, University of London, UK.

Bradley, C., Gamsu, D.S., Moses, J.L., Knight, G., Boulton, A.J.M., Drury, J., & Ward, J.D. (1987). The use of diabetes-specific perceived control and health belief measures to predict treatment choice and efficacy in a feasibility study of continuous subcutaneous insulin infusion pumps. *Psychology and Health, 1,* 133–146.

Breakwell, G.M., Hammond, S., & Fife-Schaw, C. (Eds). (1994). *Research methods in psychology.* London: Sage.

Brenner, M., Brown, J., & Canter, D. (1985). *The research interview: Uses and approaches.* London: Academic Press.

British Psychological Society. (1998). *Certificate of Competence in Occupational Testing (Level A): General Information Pack.* Leicester, UK: Author.

British Psychological Society Steering Committee on Test Standards. (1992). *Psychological testing: A guide.* Leicester, UK: British Psychological Society.

British Psychological Society Steering Committee on Test Standards. (1995). *Psychological testing: A user's guide.* Leicester, UK: British Psychological Society.

British Psychological Society Steering Committee on Test Standards. (1999). *Non-evaluative UK test publisher's list.* Leicester, UK: Author.

Brown, G.W., & Harris, T.O. (1978). *The social origins of depression.* London: Tavistock.

Brown, L.B. (1994). *The human side of prayer: The psychology of praying.* Birmingham, AL: Religious Education Press.

Burns, M.S.A. (1974). Life styles for women: An attitude scale. *Psychological Reports, 35,* 227–230.

Burns, R.B. (1979). *The self-concept in theory, measurement, development and behaviour.* London: Longman.

Buros Institute of Mental Measurement. (1992). *The 11th mental measurements yearbook* (J.J. Kramer & J.C. Conoley, Eds). Highland Park, NJ: Gryphon Press.

[Note that earlier editions of the yearbook may be needed to obtain complete information on any given test.]

Cattell, R.B. (1946). *The scientific analysis of personality*. Baltimore: Penguin.

Cattell, R.B. (1965). *The scientific analysis of personality*. Baltimore: Penguin.

Cattell, R.B., Eber, H.W., & Tatsuoka, M.M. (1970). *The 16 Personality Factor (16PF) Test*. Champaign, IL: Institute for Personality and Ability Testing.

Clark-Carter, D. (1997). *Doing quantitative psychology research: From design to report*. Hove, UK: Psychology Press.

Cohen, J. (1988). *Statistical power analysis for the behavioural sciences* (2nd ed.). Hillsdale, NJ: Lawrence Erlbaum & Associates Inc.

Cohen, J. (1992). A power primer. *Psychological Bulletin, 112*, 155–159.

Cohen, R. (1999). *Psychological testing* (4th ed.). Boston: Houghton Mifflin.

Cook, M. (1993). *Levels of personality*. London: Cassell Educational.

Coolican, H. (1999). *Research methods and statistics in psychology* (3rd ed.). London: Hodder & Stoughton.

Coopersmith, S. (1967). *The antecedents of self esteem*. San Francisco: Freeman.

Cramer, D. (1993). *Introducing statistics for social research: Step-by-step calculations and computer techniques using SPSS*. London: Taylor & Francis.

Cronbach, L. (1951). Coefficient alpha and the internal structure of tests. *Psychometrika, 16*, 297–334.

Crowne, D., & Marlowe, D. (1960). A new scale of social desirability independent of psychopathology. *Journal of Consulting Psychology, 24*, 349–354.

David, J.P. (1999). Structure of prayer scale. In P.C. Hill & R.W. Hood, Jr. (Eds), *Measures of religiosity*. Birmingham, AL: Religious Education Press.

Dawidowicz, L.S. (1977). *The Jewish presence: Essays on identity and history*. New York: Holt, Rinehart & Winston.

De Vaus, D.A. (1993). *Surveys in social research* (3rd ed.). London: UCL Press.

Dobson, K.S., Shaw, B.F., & Vallis, T.M. (1985). Reliability of a measure of the quality of cognitive therapy. *British Journal of Clinical Psychology, 24*, 295–300.

Edwards, A.L. (1957). *The social desirability variable in personality assessment and research*. New York: Dryden.

Elliott, C.D. (1983). *The British Ability Scales*. Slough, UK: National Foundation for Educational Research.

Ellis, H. (1898). Auto-eroticism: A psychological study. *Alienist and Neurologist, 19,* 260–299.

Emery, G., Hollon, S.D., & Bedrosian, R.C. (1981). *New directions in cognitive therapy: A casebook.* New York: Guilford Press.

Emmons, R.A. (1984). Factor analysis and construct validity of the Narcissistic Personality Inventory. *Journal of Personality Assessment, 48,* 291–300.

English, H.B., & English, A.C. (1958). *A comprehensive dictionary of psychological and psychoanalytical terms.* New York: Longmans, Green.

Eysenck, H.J. (1952). *The scientific study of personality.* London: Routledge & Kegan Paul.

Eysenck, H.J., & Eysenck, S.B.G. (1964). *The Eysenck Personality Inventory.* London: Hodder & Stoughton.

Eysenck, H.J., & Eysenck, S.B.G. (1975). *Manual of the Eysenck Personality Questionnaire.* San Diego, CA: Edits.

Field, A. (2000). *Discovering statistics using SPSS for Windows: Advanced techniques for beginners.* London: Sage.

Fitts, W. (1964). *The Tennessee Self-Concept Scale.* Nashville, TN: Counsellor Recordings and Tests.

Foster, J.J. (1993). *Starting SPSS-PC+ and SPSS for Windows.* Wilmslow, UK: Sigma Press.

Franken, I.R. (1988). Sensation seeking, decision making styles, and preference for individual responsibility. *Personality and Individual Differences, 9,* 139–146.

Freud, S. (1957). On narcissism: An introduction. In J. Strachey (Ed. & Trans.), *The standard edition of the complete psychological works of Sigmund Freud, Vol. 14.* London: Hogarth Press. (Original work published 1914)

Freud, S. (1961). The ego and the id. In J. Strachey (Ed. & Trans.), *The standard edition of the complete psychological works of Sigmund Freud, Vol. 19.* London: Hogarth Press. (Original work published 1923)

Furnham, A. (1984). The Protestant Work Ethic. *European Journal of Social Psychology, 14,* 87–104.

Given, C.W., Given, B.A., Gallin, R.S., & Condon, J.W. (1983). Development of scales to measure beliefs of diabetic patients. *Research in Nursing and Health, 6,* 127–141.

Glock, C.Y., Selznick, G.J., & Spaeth, J.L. (1966). *The apathetic majority: A study based on public responses to the Eichmann trial.* New York: Harper & Row.

Glock, C.Y., & Stark, R. (1966). *Christian beliefs and anti-semitism.* New York: Harper Torchbooks.

Glock, C.Y., Wuthnow, R., Piliavin, J.A., & Spencer, M. (1975). *Adolescent prejudice.* New York: Harper & Row.

Goldberg, L.R. (1990). An alternative "description of personality": The

Big-Five factor structure. *Journal of Personality and Social Psychology*, *59*, 1216–1229.

Goldman, B.A., & Mitchell, D.F. (1997). *Directory of unpublished experimental mental measures: Vol. 7.* Washington, DC: American Psychological Association.

Gravetter, F.J., & Wallnau, L.B. (1999). *Statistics for the behavioural sciences* (5th ed.). Wadsworth.

Gregory, R.J. (1996). *Psychological testing: History, principles and applications* (2nd ed.). Boston: Allyn & Bacon

Groth-Marnat, G. (1997). *Handbook of psychological assessment.* New York: Wiley.

Hathaway, S.R., & McKinley, J.C. (1943). *The Minnesota Multiphasic Personality Inventory.* Minneapolis, MN: NCS Interpretive Scoring Systems, University of Minnesota.

Hathaway, S.R., & McKinley, J.C. (1967). *The Minnesota Multiphasic Personality Inventory* (Rev. ed.). New York: Psychological Corporation.

Haynes, S. (1978). The relationship of psychosocial factors to coronary heart disease in the Framingham Study 1: Methods and risk factors. *American Journal of Epidemiology*, *107*, 362–383.

Heim, A.W. (1968). *Group Test of High Grade Intelligence AH5.* Slough, UK: National Foundation for Educational Research.

Heim, A.W. (1970). *Group Test of General Intelligence AH4.* Slough, UK: National Foundation for Educational Research.

Heim, A.W., Watts, K.P., & Simmons, V. (1983). *Group Tests of High Level Intelligence.* Slough, UK: National Foundation for Educational Research.

Higginbotham, J.B., & Cox, K.K. (1979). *Focus group interviews: A reader.* Chicago: American Marketing Association.

Hill, P.C., & Hood, R.W., Jr. (Eds). (1999). *Measures of religiosity.* Birmingham, AL: Religious Education Press.

Holmes, T.H., & Rahe, R.H. (1967). The social readjustment rating scale. *Journal of Psychosomatic Research*, *11*, 213–218.

Hood, R.W., Jr. (1975). The construction and preliminary validation of a measure of reported mystical experience. *Journal for the Scientific Study of Religion*, *14*, 29–41.

Howitt, D., & Cramer, D. (2000). *First steps in research and statistics.* London: Taylor and Francis.

Institute of Personnel and Development. (1997). *The IPD guide on psychological testing.* Wimbledon, UK: Author.

Institute of Personnel Management. (1993). IPM code on psychological testing. London: Institute of Personnel Management.

Jackson, C. (1996). *Understanding psychological testing.* Leicester, UK: British Psychological Society.

Jenkins, C.D., Zyzanski, S.J., & Rosenman, R.H. (1978). Coronary-prone behaviour: One pattern or several? *Psychosomatic Medicine, 40*, 25–43.

Jenkins, C.D., Zyzanski, S.J., & Rosenman, R.H. (1979). *Jenkins Activity Survey Form C: Manual.* San Antonio, TX: The Psychological Corporation/Harcourt Brace Jovanovitch.

Johnson, C., & Blinkhorn, S. (1994). Desperate measures: Job perform-ance and personality test measures. *The Psychologist, 7*, 167–170.

Jung, C.G. (1923). *Psychological types.* New York: Harcourt.

Kanner, A.D., Coyne, J.C., Schaefer, C., & Lazarus, R.S. (1981). Com-parison of two modes of stress measurement: Daily hassles and uplifts versus major life events. *Journal of Behavioural Medicine, 4*, 1–39.

Kaplan, R.M., & Saccuzzo, D.P. (2000). *Psychological testing: Principles, applications, and issues* (5th ed.). New York: Thomson Learning.

Kendall, I., Jenkinson, J., de Lemos, M., & Clancy, D. (1994). *Guidelines for the use of psychological tests.* Carlton South, Victoria, Australia: Australian Psychological Society Limited.

Kish, L. (1965). *Survey sampling.* New York: Wiley.

Kline, P. (1986). *A handbook of test construction.* London: Methuen.

Kline, P. (1993). *The handbook of psychological testing.* London: Routledge.

Kline, P. (1999). *The handbook of psychological testing* (2nd ed.). London: Routledge.

Krueger, R.A. (1994). *Focus groups: A practical guide for applied research.* London: Sage.

Levinson, H. (1973). Activism and powerful others: distinction within the concept of internal–external control. *Journal of Personality Assessment, 38*, 377–383.

Likert, R.A. (1932). A technique for the measurement of attitudes. *Archives of Psychology, 140*, 40–53.

Loewenthal, K.M. (1996). *An introduction to psychological tests and scales.* London: UCL Press.

Luckow, A., Ladd, K.L., Spilka, B., McIntosh, D.N., Parks, C., & LaForett, D. (1997). *The structure of prayer.* Unpublished manuscript, University of Denver, Denver, CO.

Maltby, J., Lewis, C.A., & Hill, A. (Eds). (2000). *A handbook of psycho-logical tests.* Lampeter, UK: Edwin Mellen Press.

Marx, G.T. (1967). *Protest and prejudice: A study of belief in the black community.* New York: Harper & Row.

Maton, K. (1989). The stress-buffering role of spiritual support. *Journal for the Scientific Study of Religion, 28*, 310–323.

McCracken, G. (1988). *The long interview.* Newbury Park, CA: Sage.

McCrae, R.R., & Costa, P.T. (1985). Updating Norman's "adequate taxonomy": Intelligence and personality dimensions in natural language and in questionnaires. *Journal of Personality and Social Psychology, 32,* 199–204.

Medical Research Council. (1992). *Responsibility in investigations on human participants and material on personal information.* London: Author.

Melzack, R. (1975). The McGill Pain Questionnaire: Major properties and scoring methods. *Pain, 1,* 277–299.

Morgan, D.L. (1988). *Focus groups as qualitative research.* London: Sage.

Myers, I.B., & McCaulley, M.H. (1985). *A guide to the development and use of the Myers-Briggs Type Indicator.* Palo Alto, CA: Consulting Psychologists Press.

Nunnally, J. (1978). *Psychometric theory.* New York: McGraw-Hill.

Peters, T.J., & Waterman, R.H., Jr. (1982). *In search of excellence.* New York: Warner.

Pierce, G.R., Sarason, I.G., & Sarason, B.R. (1991). General and relationship-based perceptions of social support: Are two constructs better than one? *Journal of Personality and Social Psychology, 61,* 1028–1039.

Power, M.J., Champion, L.A., & Aris, S.J. (1988). The development of a measure of social support: The Significant Others (SOS) Scale. *British Journal of Clinical Psychology, 27,* 349–358.

Raskin, R., & Hall, C.S. (1979). A Narcissistic Personality Inventory. *Psychological Reports, 45,* 590.

Raskin, R., & Terry, H. (1988). A principle-components analysis of the Narcissistic Personality Inventory and further evidence of its construct validity. *Journal of Personality and Social Psychology, 34,* 890–902.

Raven, J., Raven, J.C., & Court, J.H. (1978). *Raven's Progressive Matrices.* Oxford, UK: Oxford Psychologists' Press.

Raven, J., Raven, J.C., & Court, J.H. (1993). *Raven's Progressive Matrices* (2nd ed.). Oxford, UK: Oxford Psychologists' Press.

Robinson, J.P., Shaver, P., & Wrightsman, L.S. (Eds). (1991). *Measures of personality and social psychological attitudes.* New York: Academic Press.

Rogers, C. (1957). The necessary and sufficient conditions of therapeutic personality change. *Journal of Consulting Psychology, 21,* 95–103.

Rokeach, M. (1969). Value systems and religion. *Review of Religious Research, 11,* 2–23.

Rosenberg, S. (1965). *Society and the adolescent self-image.* Princeton, NJ: Princeton University Press.

Rosenberg, S. (1989). *Society and the adolescent self-image* (2nd ed.). Princeton, NJ: Princeton University Press.

Rotter, J.B. (1966). Generalized expectancies of internal versus external control of reinforcement. *Psychological Monographs, 80*(1, Whole No. 609).

Royal Holloway University of London. (1988). *Ethical committee notes for guidance*. London: Author.

Ryckman, R.M. (1993). *Theories of personality*. Pacific Grove, CA: Brooks/Cole.

Selznick, G., & Steinberg, S. (1969). *The tenacity of prejudice: Antisemitism in contemporary America*. New York: Harper & Row.

Siegel, S., & Castellan, N.J. (1988). *Non-parametric statistics for the behavioural sciences*. New York: McGraw-Hill.

Silver, N.C., & Hittner, J.B. (1998). *A guidebook of statistical software for the social and behavioural sciences*. Boston: Allyn & Bacon.

Smith, J. (1973). A quick measure of achievement motivation. *British Journal of Social and Clinical Psychology*, *12*, 137–143.

Stark, R., Foster, D.B., Glock, C.Y., & Quinley, H.E. (1971). *Wayward shepherds: Prejudice and the Protestant clergy*. New York: Harper & Row.

Swetland, R.C., Keyser, D.J., & O'Connor, W.A. (1983). *Tests*. Kansas City, KS: Test Corporation of America.

Tabachnick, B.G., & Fidell, L.S. (1996). *Using multivariate statistics* (3rd ed.). New York: Harper & Row.

Thurstone, L.L. (1931). The measurement of social attitudes. *Journal of Abnormal and Social Psychology*, *26*, 249–269.

Truax, C.B., & Carkhuff, R.R. (1967). *Toward effective counselling and psychotherapy*. Chicago: Aldine.

Wechsler, D. (1955). *The Wechsler Adult Intelligence Scale*. New York: Psychological Corporation.

West, R. (1991). *Computing for psychologists*. Chur, Switzerland: Harwood Academic Publishers.

Wilson, G.D., & Patterson, J.R. (1968). A new measure of conservatism (C). *British Journal of Social and Clinical Psychology*, *7*, 164–269.

Zigmond, A.S., & Snaith, R.P. (1983). The Hospital Anxiety and Depression Scale. *Acta Psychiatrica Scandinavica*, *67*, 361–370.

Zuckerman, M., & Lubin, B. (1963). *The Multiple Affect Adjective Check List*. San Diego, CA: Edits.

Useful web sites

Information on tests and psychometrics

Useful textbook

http://psychology.wadsworth.com/book/gravetterwallnau5e/index.html
This web site is associated with Gravetter and Wallnau's (1999) research methods and statistics text. It includes a very user-friendly introduction to reliability and validity.

Resources for psychologists

www.york.ac.uk/inst/ctipsych
The CTI web site is a huge repository of resources for psychology students and teachers. Among its many facilities is a search engine for statistics packages, and access to the Buros website (see next). The CTI web site is due to be dismantled, but when this happens there should be a link to a new site.

Information for test users

http://www.unl.edu/buros/
The Buros web site, which has a search engine (see the ERIC/AE test locator, next) for psychological measures, mainly covering US-published, commercially available psychometric measures, and other useful information about psychometric tests and testing.

Test locator

http://ericae.net/testcol.htm
The ERIC/AE test locator, on the Buros web site, also accessible via the CTI web site (see earlier). Lots of information about tests and test standards, with a search engine.

Handbook of psychological tests

http://handbook.infm.ulst.ac.uk/handbook.htm
The web site for Maltby, Lewis, and Hill's (2000) *Handbook of Psychological Tests*. It lists the tests covered in the handbook (all are post-1990), and gives reviews of some.

Applied Psychometrics Society

http://www.fordham.edu/aps
Web site of the Applied Psychometrics Society. Some information about psychometrics.

Intelligence and giftedness

http://maxpages.com/raindrops/Psychology_tests
Much information about psychometrics with particular emphasis on the assessment of intelligence and giftedness.

Two commercial websites

http://www.psychometrics.co.uk
A commercial web site with some downloadable psychometric tests.
http://www.acuitypsychometrics.com/
A commercial psychometrics web site with an online demonstration.

Other useful information

British Psychological Society

http://www.bps.org.uk/
For information about the British Psychological Society, Chartered Psychologist status, certificates in occupational testing, lists of UK test publishers, and other useful information. Or contact the Society at 48 Princess Park Road East, Leicester LE1 7DR; tel. 0116 2549568; email: mail@bos.org.uk

Scientific publications database

www.ncbi.nim.nih.gov/PubMed/
A publicly accessible web site of scientific publications, focused on medical topics.

Books database

http://bookshop.blackwell.co.uk
A publicly accessible web site of current academic books, some of which will contain useful test and test-related material. Has a search engine.

Author Index

Adorno, T.W. 105
Allport, G.W. 107
American Educational Research
 Association, American
 Psychological Association, &
 National Council on
 Measurement in Education
 86
American Psychiatric Association
 77
Anastasi, A. 2, 10, 11, 13, 14, 39,
 60, 64
Aris, S.J. 108
Arksey, H. 32
Arnkoff, D. 84
Australian Psychological Society
 Limited 116

Bartram, D. 23, 26
Batson, C.D. 107
Beck, A.T. 84, 101
Bedrosian, R.C. 84
Bem, S. 106
Blinkhorn, S. 18
Boulton, A.J.M. 112
Bradley, C. 21, 112
Breakwell, G.M. 32
Brenner, M. 32
British Psychological Society 26
British Psychological Society
 Steering Committee on Test
 Standards 5, 15, 25, 60, 88,
 91
Brown, G.W. 111

Brown, J. 32
Brown, L.B. 82
Burns, M.S.A. 106
Burns, R.B. 104
Buros Institute of Mental
 Measurement 23, 86, 91

Canter, D. 32
Carkhuff, R.R. 84
Castellan, N.J. 14
Cattell, R.B. 14, 103
Champion, L.A. 108
Clancy, D. 114, 116
Clark-Carter, D. 69, 143
Cohen, J. 47, 48
Cohen, R. 2
Condon, J.W. 112
Cook, M. 14
Coolican, H. 44, 45, 47, 120
Coopersmith, S. 104
Costa, P.T. 102
Court, J.H. 110
Cox, K.K. 33
Coyne, J.C. 111
Cramer, D. 58, 69, 143
Cronbach, L. 61
Crowne, D. 34, 113

David, J.P. 82
Dawidowicz, L.S. 21
de Lemos, M. 114, 116
De Vaus, D.A. 45, 120
Dobson, K.S. 83, 111
Drury, J. 112

Eber, H.W. 103
Edwards, A.L. 113
Elliot, C.D. 109
Ellis, H. 77
Emery, G. 84
Emmons, R.A. 78
English, A.C. xi
English, H.B. xi
Eysenck, H.J. 14, 17, 101
Eysenck, S.B.G. 17, 101

Fidell, L.S. 14, 67, 75, 138, 139, 152
Field, A. 14, 58, 67, 69, 75, 143, 152
Fife-Schaw, C. 32
Fitts, W. 104
Foster, D.B. 21
Foster, J. 23
Foster, J.J. 58
Franken, I.R. 79
Frenkel-Brunswick, E. 105
Freud, S. 77
Furnham, A. 109

Gallin, R.S. 112
Gamsu, D.S. 112
Given, B.A. 112
Given, C.W. 112
Glock, C.Y. 21
Goldberg, L.R. 102
Goldman, B.A. 23
Gravetter, F.J. 5, 10, 69, 120, 143, 163
Gregory, R.J. 2, 91
Groth-Marnat, G. 2

Hall, C.S. 78
Hammond, S. 32
Harris, T.O. 111
Hathaway, S.R. 102
Haynes, S. 105
Heim, A.W. 110
Higginbotham, J.B. 33
Hill, A. 23, 164
Hill, P.C. 24, 25, 106
Hittner, J.B. 15, 119
Hollon, S.D. 84
Holmes, T.H. 110
Hood, R.W. 24, 25, 106, 107
Howitt, D. 69

Institute of Personnel and Development 89
Institute of Personnel Management 25

Jackson, C. x, 16, 17, 24
Jenkins, C.D. 104
Jenkinson, J. 114, 116
Johnson, C. 18
Jung, C.G. 103

Kanner, A.D. 111
Kaplan, R.M. 2
Kendall, I. 114, 116
Keyser, D.J. 24
Kish, L. 45
Kline, P. x, 2, 10, 11, 12, 13, 14, 16, 60, 64
Knight, G. 112
Knight, P.T. 32
Krueger, R.A. 33

Ladd, K.L. 82
LaForett, D. 82
Lazarus, R.S. 111
Levinson, D.J. 105
Levinson, H. 108
Lewis, C.A. 23, 164
Likert, R.A. 19, 122
Lindley, P.A.A. 23, 26
Loewenthal, K.M. 15, 24, 60, 63, 119
Lubin, B. 100
Luckow, A. 82

McCaulley, M.H. 26, 103
McCracken, G. 32
McCrae, R.R. 102
McIntosh, D.N. 82
McKinley, J.C. 102
Maltby, J. 23, 164
Marlowe, D. 34, 113
Marshall, L. 23
Marx, G.T. 21
Maton, K. 107
Medical Research Council 118
Melzack, R. 112
Mitchell, D.F. 23
Morgan, D.L. 33

Moses, J.L. 112
Myers, I.B. 26, 103

Nunnally, J. 61

O'Connor, W.A. 24
Parks, C. 82
Patterson, J.R. 105
Peters, T.J. 80
Pierce, G.R. 108
Piliavin, J.A. 21
Power, M.J. 108

Quinley, H.E. 21

Rahe, R.H. 110
Raskin, R. 77, 78
Raven, J. 110
Raven, J.C. 110
Robinson, J.P. 24, 25
Rogers, C. 84
Rokeach, M. 107
Rosenberg, S. 104
Rosenman, R.H. 104
Rotter, J.B. 108
Royal Holloway University of
London 117
Rush, A.J. 84
Ryckman, R.M. 26

Saccuzzo, D.P. 2
Sanford, R.N. 105
Sarason, B.R. 108
Sarason, I.G. 108
Schaefer, C. 111
Schoenrade, P. 107
Selznick, G. 21
Selznick, G.J. 21
Shaver, P. 24, 25
Shaw, B.F. 83, 84, 111

Siegel, S. 14
Silver, N.C. 15, 119
Simmons, V. 110
Smith, J. 108
Snaith, R.P. 101
Spaeth, J.L. 21
Spencer, M. 21
Spilka, B. 82
Stark, R. 21
Steer, R.A. 101
Steinberg, S. 21
Swetland, R.C. 24

Tabachnick, B.G. 14, 67, 75, 138,
139, 152
Tatsuoka, M.M. 103
Terry, H. 77
Thurstone, L.L. 39
Truax, C.B. 84

Urbina, S. 2, 10, 12, 13, 60

Vallis, T.M. 83, 111
Ventis, W.L. 107
Vernon, P.E. 107

Wallnau, L.B. 5, 10, 69, 120, 143,
163
Ward, J.D. 112
Waterman, R.H. 80
Watts, K.P. 110
Wechsler, D. 109
West, R. 13, 14, 139, 152
Wilson, G.D. 105
Wrightsman, L.S. 24, 25
Wuthnow, R. 21

Zigmond, A.S. 101
Zuckerman, M. 100
Zyzanski, S.J. 104

Subject Index

accuracy checks 58–9, 129–30
achievement need 108–9
acquiescence response set 112
additivity 18–19
agree/disagree format 38
AH tests 110
Allport-Vernon Study of Values
  107–8
alpha coefficient of reliability 10,
  11–12, 60; SPSS for Windows
  133–4
alternate forms reliability 11
ambiguity 33–4
American Educational Research
  Association 86
American Psychological
  Association 86; guidelines 114
analysis of variance (anova) 69, 71,
  73–4; SPSS for Windows 149–51
anonymity 36
answer presentation 50–1
Applied Psychometrics Society 164
Australian Psychological Society
  guidelines 114–16
authoritarianism 105

Beck Depression Inventory (BDI)
  101
Bem Sex Role Inventory 106
Big Five personality factors 102
bivariate correlation 12
books database 164
brainstorming 32
British Ability Scales (BAS) 109

British Psychological Society:
  address 97; Certificates of
  Competence in Occupational
  Testing 26, 97–8; Steering
  Committee on Test Standards
  88–9, 91; website 164
Burns Life Styles for Women 106
Buros Institute of Mental
  Measurement 91; website 163

California F scale 105
categorical data 121–2
Certificates of Competence in
  Occupational Testing 26, 97–8
Chartered Psychologist 26
Child Psychology portfolio 95–6
children 112
coding data 53–7, 122–4
Cohen's kappa 14
cohesiveness 63
"cold-calling" 49
computerised testing 50–1
concurrent validity 17, 71–2; SPSS
  for Windows 147–8
confounded variables 74–5; SPSS
  for Windows 152–4
consent 35
conservatism 105–6
construct validity 17–18, 74
content validity 16, 33, 72
convenience sampling 44–5
convergent validity 17–18
conversations 32
Coopersmith scale 104

copyright 26, 33
"coronary-prone personality" 104–5
correlations 6–9; SPSS for Windows 147–8
covariance analysis 154
criterion validity 17, 69–71; SPSS for Windows 144–7, 149–51
Cronbach's alpha 10, 11–12, 60; SPSS for Windows 133–4
CSS 119
CSS/Statistica 15
CTI website 163

data: coding 53–7, 122–4; entering 57–8, 124–9; missing 130, 132–3; recoding 59, 126–8; retrieving 128–9; saving 128; type 120–2
database: checking 58–9, 129–30; construction 57–8, 124–9; error correction 129; "eye-balling" 59, 129; frequency checking 59, 129–30; printing 129; reverse scoring 59; saving 59, 128
debriefing 52
degrees of freedom 151
demographics 37
descriptive statistics 64, 68
dichotomous data 122
direct approach 48–9
discriminative power 20
divergent validity 18
double-barrelled statements 34

Edwards Social Desirability Scale 113
eigenvalues 139
ERIC/AE Test Locator 23, 163
ethical issues 28, 35–6, 50, 114–18
ethics committees 35, 117–18
"eye-balling" 59, 129
Eysenck Personality Questionnaire (EPQ) 101–2

F ratio 151
F scale 105
face validity 16, 33, 72–3
factor analysis 11, 13–14, 65–7; SPSS for Windows 138–42

factor loading 13 141–2
"faking good" 16
feedback 52, 116
focus groups 33
follow-up 52
forced-choice 38, 61–2
Framingham Anger Measure 105
frequency checking 59, 129–30

giftedness 164
group discussions 33
group testing 51
guidelines 86–91, 114–18
Guttman's coefficients 13

handbooks 164
Hassles and Uplifts Scale 111
health beliefs 112
health measures 111–12
Health Psychology Portfolio 93–5
Heim tests 110
Her Majesty's Stationery Office 91
Holmes-Rahe Social Readjustment Scale 110–11
Hospital Anxiety and Depression Scale (HAD) 101

Individual Responsibility Measure (IR) 79–81
Institute of Personnel and Development 89–91
institutions, recruiting participants through 49–50
intelligence 109–10, 164
internal consistency 11–13
inter-rater reliability 11, 14
interval data 120, 121
interval measurement 19–20
interviewee xi–xii
interviews 32–3
item: checking 33–5; mean 5, 64; numbers 32; sources 32–3; total correlations 10; weighting 39, 64, 66–7

Jenkins Activity Survey 104–5
journal databases 22–3

Kendall's coefficient of
    concordance 14
Kuder-Richardson (K-R 20) 12,
    60–1, 122

legal issues 28, 35–6
Levinson scale 108
lie scales 113
Life Events and Difficulties
    Schedule 11
Likert scale 19–20, 37–8, 122
locus of control 108, 112
logistic regression 153–4
loglinear analysis 152–3

McGill Pain Questionnaire (MPQ)
    111–12
mail shots 49
manuals 87
Marlowe-Crowne Social
    Desirability Inventory 34, 113
means 4–5
measures see tests
Measures of Religiosity 107
medical research 118
Medical Research Council 118
Mental Health Portfolio 92–3
Minnesota Multiphasic Personality
    Inventory (MMPI) 102–3, 113
missing data 130, 132–3
mood 100–5
Multiple Affect Adjective Check
    List (MAACL) 100
multiple regression analysis 154
Myers-Briggs Type Indicator
    (MBTI) 26, 103

name variables 126
naming factors 141–2
Narcissistic Personality Inventory
    (NPI) 77–9
National Council on Measurement
    in Education 86
National Foundation for
    Educational Research (NFER)
    portfolios 22, 25, 92–6
need achievement 108–9
nominal data 121–2
non-parametric statistics 120

norms xi, 4–5, 64, 68
number scale 57, 120

occcupational testing 90;
    Certificates of Competence 26,
    97–8
offensiveness 27, 34–5
one-way analysis of variance 69, 71,
    73–4; SPSS for Windows 149–51
open-ended qualitative interviews
    32–3
opportunity sampling 44–5
opting-in/opting-out 36, 50
ordered/ordinal data 120–1

parametric statistics 120
participants xi; debriefing 52;
    identification 36; recruitment
    48–50; thanking 52; withdrawal
    36, 50
Pearson correlation 12
personality 100–5
physical contact 115
point biserial correlation 122
predictive validity 17, 73–4; SPSS
    for Windows 149–51
principal components analysis 11,
    14, 65–6; SPSS for Windows
    138–42
printing 129
probability 9, 145, 147
projective tests 104
Protestant Work Ethic 109
PsychInfo 22–3
psychopathology 100–5
psychotherapy 111
publishers of tests 24, 25, 91–2

Quality of Cognitive Therapy Scale
    (CTS) 83–5
Quality of Life 112
Quality of Relationships Inventory
    (QRI) 108
QUALPRO 15
quasi-random sampling 44
quotas 44

random sampling 43, 44
range 4–5

rating scales 122
Raven's Progressive Matrices 110
recoding 59, 126–8
recruitment 48–50
redundancy 17
reliability 5–9; assessment 9–11, 133–4; defined 5; improvement 62–4, 135–7; SPSS for Windows 133–7; statistics 11–15, 59–62
religion 106–7
religious experience measure 107
Religious Life Inventory 107
respondent xi-xii
response: biases 112; format 37–41; rate 46–7
retrieval 128–9
reverse meaning 34, 55–6, 59, 126–7
reverse scoring 59
Rokeach checklist 107
Rorschach test 26, 104
Rosenberg scale 104
rotation methods 138–9
Rotter scale 108
Royal Holloway University of London, ethical committee guidelines 117–18

sample/sampling 4, 28, 42–8; bias 44–5, 46, 47; error 9; methods 43–5; size 47–8
SAS 15
SAS/STAT 14, 15, 119
saving data 128
scale 18 see also tests
scaling xi, 19
scientific publications database 164
self-esteem 104
sex roles 106
Significant Others Scale (SOS) 108
Sixteen Personality Factors Questionnaire (16PF) 103
Smith scale 108–9
snowball sampling 45
social attitudes and cognitions 105–9

social desirability 34, 112–13
social support 108
spiritual support 107
split-half reliability 10–11, 12, 61, 63
spoken answers 51
SPSS 15; factor and principal components analysis 14
SPSS for Windows 119; analysis of variance 149–51; correlations 147–8; covariance analysis 154; database construction and checking 124–33; entering data 124–9; error correction 129; factor analysis 138–42; frequency checking 130; importing files 57; logistic regression 153–4; loglinear analysis 152–3; missing data replacement 133; multiple regression analysis 154; principal components analysis 138–42; printing 129; reliability analysis 133–4; reliability improvement 135–7; retrieving data 128–9; saving data 128; t-test 144–7; total scores 143–4; validity checking 143–54
SPSS-PC 15, 119
SPSS-X 15, 119
standard deviation 4–5
standardisation 2, 64
Standards for Educational and Psychological Test 86–8
Stanford-Binet test 109
statistical power 47–8
statistics packages 15, 119
stratified sampling 44
stress 110–11
Structure of Prayer Scale 82–3
subjects xi
SYSTAT 15, 119

t-test 69–71, 73; SPSS for Windows 144–7
target group 44
telephone recruitment 49
Tennessee Self-Concept Scale 104
test-retest reliability 10, 12

testee xi; qualifications and training 26–7
testing xi; guidelines 86–91, 114–18
tests: administering 28, 50–1; defined xi; examples 77–85, 98–113; existing, pros and cons of using 28; key features 2–20, 25; locating 22–7, 163; manuals 87; presentation 75–6; selection 86–113; standards 86–9; user restrictions 26–7, 99; writing 30–41
textbooks 163
texts, quoting from 33
thanking participants 52
total scores 57; SPSS for Windows 143–4
training 26
two-way analysis of variance, SPSS for Windows 151
Type A behaviour 104–5

validity 15–18, 68–75; SPSS for Windows 143–54
value variables 126
values measures 107–8
varimax 138–9
visual analogue scale 38, 56

Web of Science 22–3
web sites 163–4
Wechsler Adult Intelligence Scale (WAIS) 109
weighting 39, 64, 66–7
Wilson-Patterson C scale 105–6
withdrawal from test 36, 50
wording of tests 6
writing tests 30–41
written answers 50–1

yea-saying 34, 112
yes/no format 38